Perchance to Dream

The World of
IVOR NOVELLO

Perchance
to Dream

Richard Rose

Leslie Frewin of London

B

First published 1974 by

Leslie Frewin Publishers Limited,
Five Goodwin's Court,
Saint Martin's Lane,
London WC2N 4LL, England

Designed by Craig Dodd

This book is set in Garamond Bold
Photoset, printed and bound in Great Britain by
Weatherby Woolnough, Sanders Road,
Wellingborough, Northamptonshire

ISBN 0 85632 120 6

'. . . to die, to sleep,

      to sleep, perchance to dream

   Ay, there's the rub

For in that sleep of death what dreams may come . . .'

—WILLIAM SHAKESPEARE

Acknowledgements

I owe a deep debt of gratitude to many friends and to several firms for their help, and for the use of copyright photographs.

I would particularly like to thank Stephen Watts for his editorial help, and Olive Gilbert, who loaned Leslie Frewin many of her precious collection of photographs of Ivor.

I must also thank Geoffrey Hann and Eric Braun for their valuable assistance.

Despite diligent effort, I have been unable to trace the copyright of several photographs and if I have unwittingly erred, I apologise. I acknowledge with gratitude photographs by Sir Cecil Beaton, Anthony Buckley, Paul Tanqueray, Tom Hustler and Camera Press, Foulsham and Bamfield, Aracil (Madrid), Keystone Press, Humphrey and Vera Joel, Alexander Bender, the Angus McBean-Harvard Theatre Collection, The Stage Photo Company, Mander and Mitchenson Collection, Dorothy Wilding, *Picturegoer* Series, Landseer of London, *Daily Telegraph*, J. Beagles, Sasha, W. Gordon Davis, Gerald Murison and The National Film Archive.

Jacket and Frontispiece photograph by Anthony Buckley.

Contents

Illustrations

53. – 56. *Opposite top left:* Ivor in *Murder In Mayfair,* 1934, *top right:* Edna Best, *bottom right:* Fay Compton, *bottom left:* Zena Dare, all in *Murder In Mayfair.*
57. Ivor and Mary Ellis in *Glamorous Night,* 1935.
58. Ivor Novello *c* 1945.
59. Ivor and Mary Ellis in another scene from *Glamorous Night,* 1935.
60. The Ballroom Scene from *Glamorous Night.*
61. Isabel Jeans and Dorothy Hyson, daughter of Dorothy Dickson in Oscar Wilde's *Lady Windemere's Fan.*
62. Ivor and Isabel Jeans in the early movie, *Downhill.*
63. Ivor and Isabel Jeans in Clemence Dane's *The Happy Hypocrite,* His Majesty's Theatre, 1936.
64. Ivor and Vivien Leigh in a dramatic scene from *The Happy Hypocrite.*
65. Vivien Leigh.
66. Dorothy Dickson and Ivor in *Careless Rapture.*
67. The memorable Rose Ballet from *Careless Rapture* designed by René Hubert.
68. Ivor in the name role and Dorothy Dickson as Katharine of France in Shakespeare's *Henry V,* Drury Lane Theatre, 1938.
69. Ivor and Vanessa Lee in *King's Rhapsody.*
70. Ivor and Vanessa Lee immediately after her success on the first night of *King's Rhapsody,* 1950.
71. Olive Gilbert, one of Ivor's closest friends and co-stars, seen here with the actor-playwright-composer in *Perchance To Dream.*
72. Ivor's favourite portrait of himself – from *King's Rhapsody.*
73. The finale of *The Dancing Years.*
74. Ivor (left) on holiday at his Jamaican home with (next to him) Zena Dare (below), Olive Gilbert, Bobbie Andrews and (top right) two other friends.
75. Bobby Andrews, Ivor, Lord Beaverbrook and Beatrice Lillie at Ivor's home in Jamaica. It was Ivor's last holiday . . .
76. Ivor Novello (left) arrives at the London Law Courts on 16th May, 1944 to hear his appeal against his conviction of eight weeks' imprisonment for conspiring to commit an offence against restriction on the war-time use of cars. His appeal failed. Many considered it a cruel and unjust sentence.
77. Ivor Novello on his release from prison on 12th June 1944. He resumed his starring role in *The Dancing Years* at the Adelphi Theatre, London on 20th June.
78. The exterior of 'Redroofs', Ivor's famous home near Maidenhead, Berkshire.
79. Ivor in the pool at 'Redroofs' – standing in swimsuit (right) is actor Peter Graves, now Lord Graves, who married one of Ivor's leading ladies, Vanessa Lee.
80. A bathing party at 'Redroofs'. Ivor (sitting second from right), always the most generous of hosts, with some of his friends round the pool of his Berkshire home.
81. Ivor at a window of 'Redroofs'.
82. (l to r) Ivor, Alan Melville, another friend and Bobbie Andrews at 'Redroofs', 4th March 1951. He died two days later.

Foreword

When I came to London from America in 1931 to be associated with Ivor Novello in the production of his plays, I had the good fortune not only to present many of his successful comedies but also to be included in his circle of close friends.

I have recorded in this book some of my happy memories of Ivor, his friends, and his life on and off the stage during the years I spent in England.

In the first part of the book I have touched briefly on his early life and successes which he recounted to me in detail and which, I feel, form a necessary background to what follows.

Madrid, 1974   RR

1
Early
Triumphs

IVOR

IVOR NOVELLO WAS the most romantic actor of his time and probably the best-loved man in the English theatre. Even today the mention of his name, or the sound of one of the scores of songs he composed, will flood with nostalgia the hearts and minds of a multitude of people who hold his memory dear.

His generosity to everyone, and especially to people of the theatre when they needed help in difficult moments of their lives, was well-known. He had a great love for his fellow humans and an endearing desire to share with them his happiness and his success. He had a highly individual brand of charm, on and off the stage, which captivated all who knew him as well as his audiences.

His creative gifts were brilliant, his wit exceptional and – on top of all that – such good looks that thousands of women fell in love with him.

Yet with all the affection and popularity that he attracted he remained completely unspoiled; praise and applause never went to his head; in any case, his sense of humour would always have saved him from the danger of conceit.

Complacency was unknown to him. He was always striving to write better plays and to give better performances so that he could reach the goal he had set for himself in the theatre. He was proud of his Welsh heritage, and grateful to it, as it accounted for so much of his enthusiasm, his fantasy, his passion for music, and a certain romantic and mystic quality with which he was imbued.

The theatre was his first and greatest love, although it would seem that he will be best remembered for his music. From the time he was taken as a little boy by his mother to matinées to see pantomimes and children's plays he was enraptured and spellbound by everything he saw on the stage; as he grew up he became more and more enthralled by the theatre and saved all the money he could to go to the Gaiety, Daly's, the Strand and especially to his favourite, Drury Lane, where musicals and melodrama thrilled him equally.

16

He saw the beautiful and famous actresses of the turn of the century and fell in love with Lily Elsie in *The Merry Widow* which he saw more than twenty times. He saw Gertie Millar in *The Quaker Girl* and Zena and Phyllis Dare in all their musicals. He longed to write plays of his own for them, and even dared to hope that perhaps one day he might play the romantic parts opposite them. This ambition became so great that he made up his mind that nothing in the world would stop him from achieving it.

*   *   *

Ivor's secretary kept in his desk a list of people to whom cheques were sent each month. The first half was the permanent list, which was made up of old actors and actresses whom Ivor had known from his early days in the theatre and films. They had retired but though they had small pensions they could not have carried on without his help.

The second part of the list was the temporary one in which were the names of theatre people out of work at the moment, often because of illness, who would return to the stage as soon as they were well and able to find work again. The size of this list was always changing, but it never seemed to become smaller as there were always new names to replace the old ones; indeed, and unfortunately, the list grew, because of the vicissitudes of the theatre.

One day when Ivor's secretary was reporting the latest box office receipts of the current show he seemed very worried and asked Ivor if he had any idea of the amount of money he had given away in the last few months.

'No,' said Ivor, 'and I don't want to hear anything about it. Those poor souls are depending on what I send them and I'll never let them down. Thank heaven I can earn enough to take care of the darlings. Cut down on any other expenses if you have to, but never on those cheques.'

Ivor's kindness and sympathy seemed to draw out the best qualities in people. Everyone loved working with him and his companies were always happy ones, with Ivor – irrespective of ages – as the father figure. He knew everyone's ability and what kind of a performance he could expect them to give. He also knew about their personal lives and no matter how busy he was they always felt free to go to his dressing-room to tell him about their worries and problems, hoping that he could resolve them, which he usually did.

He epitomised 'star quality'. From the moment he walked on to the stage the eyes of his audiences were riveted on him, and his personality (plus his charm and good looks) kept them enthralled to the end. Off-stage it was little different. He had only to appear in a restaurant or hotel, indeed in any public place, to attract immediately the attention of everyone there, and without the slightest effort on his part. He seemed to possess a magnetism that drew people close to him; many famous actors and playwrights have been known to the public by their full names or surnames but he was 'Ivor' to the many who knew him personally and the millions who didn't. These were not foolish fans of any particular class or age-group. A business-man would tell his wife that he had bought two stalls for 'Ivor's new play at the Globe'; the barman in the pub opposite Drury Lane would say to his customers: 'Ivor's got another full house over there tonight.' They all spoke of him as if he were a friend they had known all their lives.

*   *   *

Ivor always maintained that he had no great message to give to the people who came to see his plays. 'I just want to give them good entertainment,' he said. The proof that he achieved this was confirmed by the frequency with which the 'Full House' and 'Standing Room Only' signs appeared outside the theatre where he was acting.

Ivor was a great romantic who, from the overture onwards, led his audiences into a mythical, magical world of enchantment, of glamorous people, of song and dance and spectacle. He also wanted the world around him to be as colourful and as glamorous as the one he created on the stage. His enthusiasm and *joie de vivre* helped him to a great extent

18

to make this come true. When at times he was faced with some of the unpleasant realities of life he did his utmost to resolve them and then, having erased them from his mind, he quickly forgot that they had ever happened. He could always take refuge in composing or writing for the theatre that he loved so much and thus escape from the world of reality. He was happiest when he was working in the theatre, and especially when he was acting in one of his own plays.

*   *   *

A memorial plaque to mark the twenty-first anniversary of Ivor Novello's death was unveiled in St Paul's Cathedral. It was a solemn moment for the multitudes of his followers who attended the service. Two months later a Gala Sunday Night Performance at Drury Lane was given in his memory and many of his most beautiful melodies were sung by famous singers. During the interval groups of people stood admiring Clemence Dane's bronze head of Ivor in the Circle Rotunda. There it stands along with the busts of Garrick, Kean and other famous artists who contributed so much to the history of this great theatre. Ivor was the only one among them, in the nearly three hundred years of its history, who had brought three great talents to Drury Lane. He wrote, composed and acted there in all of his best-remembered productions.

MAM

CLARA NOVELLO DAVIES was a fantastic woman. She was also a beautiful woman, with black, piercing eyes and a mass of blue-black hair. She had studied singing in Italy with a teacher named Novello, and had taken this name for herself thinking it more fitting for the musical career she was planning.

When she returned to Cardiff she married a kind, handsome man who worked in a government office there, and he created a solid background for his exhuberant and talented young wife. She opened a school of music in their home, giving both singing and piano lessons, and soon she had many pupils who admired the way she taught and were captivated by her charm and enthusiasm. She was always encouraging, and was given to predicting great futures for them.

Ivor was born and spent his childhood in this musical atmosphere, and his earliest recollections were of people singing around the piano, with his mother directing them. It was only natural that he developed a great love for music, and by the time he was eight years old his mother was already giving him piano and singing lessons. He would often go to the piano and pick out tunes, and soon began to write a few little songs himself. His mother was constantly at his side praising what he had written and encouraging him to continue. Her great ambition was for him to become a composer. It was because she thought Ivor Novello was a more suitable name for a composer than David Ivor Davies that she persuaded him to change his name. Ivor adored his mother and thought her the most glamorous and exciting person in the world.

The Davies household had a wide circle of visitors, many of them from the musical world, and much of the conversation centred on the concerts and music festivals of the time in England and, more especially, in Wales. David Lloyd George and his family were great friends of Ivor and his mother and Ivor wrote a song *Megan* dedicated to Lloyd George's daughter. The two families remained friends throughout the Prime Minister's lifetime and were often together at 10 Downing Street.

Inevitably some of Madame Clara's pupils went to London and through their success her fame as a teacher grew; soon she was going to London several times a month to teach singers – even stars – of the theatre who had no time to come to her in Cardiff. Ivor often accompanied her and so met many of her famous friends. Among them was the celebrated Mrs Patrick Campbell for whom Shaw had written *Pygmalion* and other of his successful plays. She loved Ivor; she chose him to be a

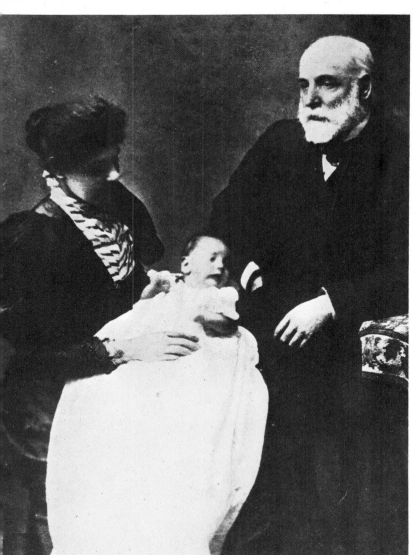

1.
Left: Mother (his beloved 'Mam'), Ivor as a baby, and his grandfather.

2.
Right: Ivor posed for his first photograph at the age of a few weeks in company with Mam, the celebrated Clara Novello Davies.

3.
Above: Ivor is seen in these two pictures as a small boy with Mam.

4.
Right: An early picture of Ivor's adored and adoring Mam.

bove: Ivor with his father, David Davies,
nd Mam.

ight: Ivor with his beloved Mam at Black-
ool, Lancs, during the provincial run of
he Dancing Years in 1945.

8.
Below: Ivor, as a young man, with his lifelong friend Bobbie Andrews.

7.
Above: Two studies of Ivor in his early twenties.

9.
Right: A drawing by dramatist Clemence Dane of Ivor in his role in *Autumn Crocus*.

10.
Above: The famous acting sisters Zena and Phyllis Dare *c* 1905.

11.
Above right: Phyllis Dare (with Page Adair) in *Cinderella c* 1906.

12.
Right: An early photograph of Zena Dare.

13.
Above: A photograph of Lily Elsie taken in the early part of the century.

14.
Above right: Ivor with Lily Elsie in *The Truth Game,* 1928.

15.
Right: Ivor with another of his leading ladies, Benita Hume.

page at her wedding and they remained great friends for the rest of her life.

Ivor's mother, whom he and his friends affectionately called 'Mam', had always dreamed of organising a choir of Welsh women and directing them in concerts throughout Britain. She began by selecting several of her pupils with exceptional voices and giving auditions to other young people in Wales. She went through difficult moments but she was a person who would never be defeated once she had made a plan – a quality Ivor inherited directly from her.

After a couple of years of hard work she had a group ready to give their first concert in Cardiff. It was a great success and before long they were singing in concert halls all over the country. The Welsh Ladies' Choir, wearing the traditional costumes of their country, became so well-known that their fame reached the ears of Queen Victoria who invited Mam to bring them to Osborne where she was spending the summer. She was delighted with their performance and bestowed on Madame Clara a jewelled medal. From then on Mam wore it from when she woke up in the morning until she retired at night whether she was in a bathrobe, an evening gown, or one of her concert costumes.

Mam dressed in one of her costumes must have been a magnificent sight. She wore beautiful gowns of gold and silver *lamé* designed by the Court dressmakers of the time. On her head she wore a golden crown with a laurel leaf design and she carried a baton with a gold handle. No entrances from the wings for her. She walked majestically down the central aisle of the auditorium, to the accompaniment of great applause, and up to the podium from which she conducted her girls.

Word of these concerts spread to America and she was invited to bring her Welsh Choir to the World Fair in Chicago to compete with singers from every country in Europe. She returned to England in triumph. She always had been a great believer in publicity. 'Without it,' she often said, 'one can never get to the top.' She cultivated friendships in the newspaper world and as she was much admired, as well as being such a colourful character, she attracted a vast amount of valuable Press publicity.

While she was in America she was approached by the impresario of the Metropolitan Opera who suggested that she take a studio in New York and give lessons to young opera aspirants. She agreed to do this and before long she was back in New York, established in a tremendous apartment in Central Park West. She engaged servants and began to give huge parties for celebrities of the musical and theatrical world, many of the leaders of New York society and, of course, the Press. The result was that so many people came to her for lessons that she could not take them all and had to have a waiting-list.

Sometimes during lessons she would rush to her bedroom and drink a quick glass of champagne. When she returned to her pupils she would be so over-enthusiastic and complimentary that they immediately saw themselves on the stage of the Metropolitan. Occasionally, on the other hand, when she did not like the way a pupil was singing, she would deliver a sharp punch in the stomach and say, 'There! That's where it should come from! Not from the throat! Now breathe deeply and begin all over again.'

In a few years she was making a great deal of money but her extravagance was boundless and she spent every penny on entertaining, on clothes, and on satisfying all her whims. She completely ignored her financial situation so she suddenly found herself deeply in debt.

A friend of Ivor's, a well-known American lawyer who had taken care of his business affairs when he was making a film for D. W. Griffith in America, sent Ivor a message about his mother's situation, adding his opinion that Ivor would have to stop her teaching and get her back to England. Ivor wrote asking how much money would be needed to settle her debts. When the answer came – fifteen thousand dollars – he sent a cheque to the lawyer, including extra money to wind up her affairs and put her on the next boat to England.

This was a terrible blow to her but she had no choice. Ivor went to Southampton to meet the boat, determined to give Clara a scolding and to run her life himself in future. When he reached the pier the boat had just arrived and the passengers were disembarking. He saw an ambulance standing near by but thought nothing of it. When at last all the passengers seemed to have left the boat and there was no sign of Mam he became frightened, and even more so, when he saw two stewards carrying a stretcher from the ship and putting it into the ambulance. He quickly asked who the sick person was and they told him that it was Madame Clara Novello Davies who had been unconscious all during the trip and was to be sent by ambulance to London.

Ivor, in a panic, climbed into the ambulance and sat beside the stretcher. He talked to her continuously, trying to bring her out of the coma, but to no avail. He was overwhelmed with sorrow and tears were pouring down his cheeks when they arrived at the clinic where she remained for a week without regaining consciousness. He spent most of the time at her bedside trying to revive her.

Suddenly, one day he said, 'Mam darling, if you will only get well I'll never mention your troubles in New York and I'll give you everything you want for the rest of your life.' As soon as he had said these words her hand suddenly began to move and reached for his, clasping it strongly. She opened her eyes and started to talk as if nothing had happened to her. They kissed and Ivor was so happy that he never mentioned her financial mess in America. He gave her a little house near Marble Arch and invited three of her Welsh women to live with her and soon she began to teach again.

When she was better she organised her 'Welsh Singing Grandmothers' Choir' which was composed largely of the women that she had conducted earlier in life and who were now in their late fifties. They all adored her because she had taken them out of their dull, monotonous lives and had given them years of excitement and achievement. Once again she gave concerts all over England but times were changing and people's musical tastes were changing too. The audiences became smaller and smaller but she was undaunted. She arranged to have all unsold seats given away to nurses, hotel employees, and even to bus and taxi drivers, so that the halls were well-filled even though very few people had paid for their seats. She never admitted this but at length even the people with free tickets didn't want to go to the concerts.

She was in her late seventies when Ivor urged her to give up her concerts and to continue only with her lessons. She was not feeling well so Ivor persuaded her to go to his house in the country and to rest for three months.

One day he said to me, 'Mam is certainly being a good girl and doing just what the doctor ordered, but she is being so quiet that I am not completely sure she's not up to something.' He could not have been more correct.

A few days later she arrived at the London flat and rushed into the bedroom where he was having breakfast. She was in top form and very excited.

'Darling,' she said, 'the most wonderful thing has happened. We're going to sing for Hitler in Berlin. I am going to take sixty of my girls with me and our slogan is going to be "Singing for Peace". We're going to start at The Hague and give two concerts in Holland and two in Belgium on our way to Berlin. When we sing for Hitler in the stadium there we're going to change from our Welsh costumes into white angel dresses for our Grand Finale and release hundreds of pigeons, each one carrying on its leg a little message of peace.'

Ivor, aghast and terrified of where this wild idea might lead, tried to calm her. But it was no good.

'Everything is arranged,' she said. 'We're leaving tomorrow. Lady Malcolm, who's always been one of my greatest fans, is going to finance the whole trip. Now darling, I've got to rush off because I have a big Press conference at the Waldorf next door ... but you'll read all about it in the papers ...'

She threw her arms around him, kissed him, and rushed out of the flat.

No more was seen or heard of her until Ivor learned that the fantastic party had actually left for Holland. There was no word from her during the first two days of the trip, then suddenly, a telegram arrived: 'Concert halls filled to capacity. Deafening applause. Greatest success of my career. On to Berlin. Send me four thousand pounds immediately.'

Ivor contacted his business manager and put in a telephone call to Amsterdam where that night's concert was to take place. He learned that the management of the opera house had decided to cancel the concert because there had been hardly any audience the night before at The Hague. The Dutch, it seemed, were not at all interested in the Welsh Singing Grandmothers. Ivor gave his secretary, Fred Allen a cheque, told him to take the next boat to Holland, pay off all the debts that had accumulated, and bring Mam and her sixty Welsh ladies back to England immediately. She was furious and put up strong resistance before she would get on the boat.

Once back in London she locked herself in her house and would not see or speak to anyone. Even when Ivor went there she refused to see him. She remained in seclusion for over a month then appeared at his house in the country and was her old vivacious self. The Hitler fiasco was never mentioned again until the week of the Munich crisis two years later. She was sitting at her window watching buildings being sand-bagged and other signs of preparations for war. She turned to one of her women and said bitterly, 'If they had let us go to Berlin all this would never have happened.'

After she had given up her concerts she still could not bear to be out of the spotlight. She decided on a new plan. As Ivor had become so famous she would more and more play a public role as the mother of Ivor Novello. She would take the royal box in the theatre where he was playing, and appear in lavish long-trained gowns carrying enormous bouquets of flowers. Her arrival in the box caused so much commotion that people in the audience would look up to see what was going on. She would then go to the front of the box and bow and throw kisses to the audience. Sometimes they would applaud loudly assuming she was some royalty – or at least celebrity – they didn't happen to know.

All this amused Ivor tremendously and although many times she made him terribly nervous he never admitted it to anyone. He would always

31

say, 'Isn't Mam marvellous? Have you ever seen anyone her age with such vitality and enthusiasm? She is absolutely incorrigible.'

One day when the three of us were sitting at Redroofs, Ivor's country house, and Mam was making a dramatic speech about one of her concerts in America, Ivor said, 'Mam, you should have been an actress. You would have put Sarah Bernhardt to shame.' It all ended in laughter.

I saw her for the last time on a very cold and rainy day in the country. It was a Monday morning and I had to go to London. Mam insisted, as always, that she come with me as her pupils were waiting for her and she had many other appointments to fulfil. She came down the path from the house to the car, her grey hair blowing in every direction, wearing a purple velvet tea-gown with the train trailing on the wet flagstones. Two silver foxes were fastened on to the dress with big safety pins and she carried a fur rug to wrap around herself in the car.

The maids were waiting at the car with large baskets of vegetables, fruit, eggs, and a chicken for her to take to her house in London. When we were settled, she asked one of the maids to open a bottle of champagne; and bring two glasses – 'So that Mr Rose and I can get warmed-up for the trip'. When they returned, she lifted her glass towards me and said, 'Here's to us, Dickie darling, and all the great things we're going to do in the future.'

She talked and laughed a great deal for the next half hour. Then slowly her eyes began to close, her voice became a whisper, and her head fell gently on to her chest. She remained in a deep sleep until we arrived at her house where her two Welsh women were waiting for her. They lifted her tenderly from the car and led her into the house, undressed her and laid her in her bed, where she would rest and dream until the next weekend when she would go to Ivor's again.

There were no pupils waiting for her and there had been none for several years. They had gone to younger and more modern teachers but she could not bear to face this reality. It would have killed her. She had to cling to the illusion that she was still living in the days of her triumphs, when her concerts were being applauded throughout England.

KEEP THE HOME FIRES BURNING

IN ENGLAND IN the latter part of 1914 – and much more widely in the later years of the First World War – it would have been difficult, if one had wanted to do so, to avoid hearing, in the course of any day, the sound of a song composed by Ivor Novello. He was twenty-one when he wrote *Keep the Home Fires Burning* and it made his name, as well as a great deal of money.

It was played everywhere, from the orchestras of smart hotels to the pianos of pubs, and by organ-grinders on the streets too. It was quickly adopted by the British Army and its chorus rang out from the troop trains leaving Victoria Station, at the French ports of disembarkation, and so on wherever British soldiers were. French soldiers learned it parrot-wise, then it was translated into French and five other languages.

It reached America in 1915, heard for the first time at the Century Theatre, New York, and greeted with a great ovation. It spread rapidly and even before the United States was in the war it was one of the most popular songs all over the country. It was more popular than *Tipperary* – the other great favourite song of that period – because words like 'Tipperary' and 'Piccadilly' were not so well-known to Americans, and most of them didn't even know how to pronounce 'Leicester Square'.

The tune and the words were easy to learn, which was exactly what Ivor had intended. I once asked him about how he came to write it.

'I wanted to write something patriotic,' he said. 'Something which would have a message of hope for the boys who were going off to war. I intended it to be emotional and sentimental, and unlike the usual war songs. After about three weeks I'd written quite a beautiful song that I thought might do, but I decided it wasn't what I wanted and put it in a revue that I was writing.

'The song I wanted to write seemed to elude me until one day at the flat, when I was looking out of the window at the black clouds racing across the sky, the music I was searching for flashed through my mind. I rushed to the piano and without any hesitation played the complete verse and chorus of it. I played it over several times to a friend of mine who had written the lyrics for some of my other songs and she was very enthusiastic about it. I wanted the words to be easy to learn and to remember. They must be about home, I decided – the homes the boys were always remembering and longing to return to when the war was over, and the families in these homes, who would be so anxiously awaiting them. I was looking around the room trying to find a clue that would help me, when the maid came in to put some wood on the fire, and I said: "That's it! That is just what I want! The fireside and the logs burning brightly."

'I went to the piano and played some bars of the new song, and then slowly, I began to sing: "Keep the home fires burning, while your hearts are yearning." You take it from there, I said to my friend.

'In half an hour she had written the words and I immediately jotted them down on paper with the music. I asked Sybil Vane, a pupil of my mother's, who had a beautiful soprano voice, to come over that evening. I used to accompany her when she sang at Sunday concerts, and I hoped that at the next one, which was to be at the Alhambra Theatre, we could introduce this piece to the public. She was enthusiastic about the song, and sang it over many times. So on Sunday we went nervously to the theatre to try it out.

'The audience was in a rather quiet mood that afternoon. The anxieties of the war had dampened their spirits and the first songs she sang, which usually went very well, had a rather cool reception. It had been announced in the programme that she would sing a new song composed by me, at the end of the concert. When the time came she sang the verse and the chorus and there was loud applause, which gave us courage to carry on. Then she sang the verse and the chorus a second time, with even more success.

'When she began to repeat the chorus again it seemed to me that I heard voices in the audience, singing it with her, and then suddenly, like magic, everyone stood up and sang the entire chorus together, applauding wildly at the end. The enthusiasm was so great that we had to repeat playing it six more times and the next day the music shops were besieged by people who wanted to buy copies of it, and I knew that I had the first great success in my career as a composer.'

THE FILM STAR

IT WAS NATURAL that with his looks and charm Ivor should attract the film producers who saw in him the romantic hero they were always searching for. He was not sure, however, that he wanted to go into films as they were a far cry from the theatre where he longed to be. Finally he decided to act in one film and see what ability he really had as an actor.

The film, *The Call of the Blood,* was made in Sicily, and his part was a very romantic one which he found no difficulty at all in playing. But when the film was shown he thought he was terrible in it. However, it turned out to be a great success, and his acting was widely praised.

After this, he was besieged by the producers, and he began to make one successful film after another. The best of these was *The Lodger*, one of the first films directed by Alfred Hitchcock and the one that established him as a director. Ivor gave a fine performance and it was shown all over the world, rated as the best British film that had been made up to that time. Ivor was voted Number One Film Star of England and Number Two Film Star of Europe, second only to the glamorous Pola Negri.

One evening, David W. Griffith, the brilliant American pioneer director, went to supper with some theatre friends at the Savoy Grill in London. He had been on a trip through the Continent, trying to find an actor to play the star part in his new picture, *The White Rose*, but had not seen anyone that he fancied.

Griffith was not only the first director to make great epic films, such as *The Birth of a Nation, Way Down East,* and *Intolerance,* but he was also a great creator. He never gave a script to any of his actors to learn, but made up the dialogue himself as he went along. Aspirants to film fame would have given everything they possessed to have been chosen to act under his direction because they knew that it was the sure road to stardom.

Shortly after Griffith arrived at the Savoy, Ivor came in with some friends for supper. Griffith scrutinized him intensely for the next half hour. He noted the features and the bone structure of his face, the way he spoke, and all of his gestures. Finally, he asked his friends: 'Who is the young man sitting at that table?'

'It's Ivor Novello,' one of them said. 'He is a very popular film star here.'

'I don't care about that,' Griffith said. 'Will you ask him to telephone me tomorrow? I want to talk to him.'

Next day Ivor went to see him at his hotel and Griffith said, 'I want you to come to America and act in my new film, *The White Rose*. There is a wonderful part for you in it. I'll send you a cable a few weeks before we start filming.'

Ivor was very impressed by the magnetism and personality of the great man, and he knew that being directed by him would be an invaluable experience. In due course the message came. Ivor said goodbye to all his friends and sailed for the United States.

When he arrived in New York the great publicity machine of Griffith's studio had already begun to work. There was a crowd of reporters and photographers at the boat to meet him and the next day his picture was in all the papers, with interviews and articles about his life and successes in England.

Gladys Cooper was staying with Ivor's mother in England at the time and a great romance between them was soon built up by the newspapers. The spotlight was constantly on them; they were described as 'the most beautiful and famous couple in the British theatre', and the oft-repeated story was that they were in love. Ivor was called 'the great English profile' and compared with Ramon Novarro, Richard Barthelmess and even with Rudolph Valentino. He found the flattery unbearable and was delighted when it was time to go to Florida and begin the film.

The picture turned out to be a success, though it wasn't one of Griffith's best, and the critics were loud in praise of Ivor. Now thousands of new fans joined those he already had in England, and he was besieged with offers to make more films in America. But he wanted to do only one thing – to return to London and the theatre he loved so much.

36.
Above: Ivor in his starring role in the early movie, *The Vortex.*

37.
Right: Star of the film, of his play, *The Lodger.*

18.
Above: Star of the early movie, *Carnival.*

19.
Right: Opposite Madeleine Carroll in
Sleeping Car.

).
bove: Ivor in a dramatic
cene from the now classic
m *The Rat.*

.
ight: Cecily Courtneidge –
or wrote *Gay's the Word* for
er.

22.
Above: Star of the successful film, *Autumn Crocus.*

23.
Left: Ivor in a scene from the film, *I Lived With You.*

Back in England, he continued to compose songs for revues and musical comedies and he had many offers from British film companies. His fan mail had grown to such proportions that he had to send off seven hundred signed photographs a week. But he also found time to write a play – *The Rat* – in collaboration with his old friend, Constance Collier, in which he wrote a strong romantic part for himself. The play, about a handsome Apache in Paris who falls in love with a beautiful Parisian aristocrat, was a thriller, and had some very clever situations in it. Ivor decided to produce it himself with his own money, and to star in it with Dorothy Batley and Isabel Jeans. 'I was the first one to put my name up in lights over a theatre,' he told me. 'Nobody else has seemed to want to do it.'

The play opened in Brighton and there were thirty curtain calls at the end. The critics gave it excellent reviews and although it was not a wonderful play it had a great appeal for audiences everywhere, especially for Ivor's fans. It was bought for a film in which he played the star part.

The masses of film fans who had idolised Ivor in his pictures rushed to see him in his play, to find out if he was as handsome and romantic in the flesh as he was on the screen. They were not disappointed, and filled the theatre at every performance, which assured a long run for the play. The matinées were especially crowded with excited women and girls, and people began to call Ivor a 'matinée idol', a term which he loathed so much that he vowed he would do everything in his power to obliterate it.

People who were envious of his success said that it was the romantic working girls who had made him their hero and were alone responsible for his enormous popularity. It was true that he received thousands of letters from girls who openly declared their love for him, told him that they covered the walls of their rooms with his photographs, and went to sleep every night with his picture under their pillows. It was understandable that his romantic image made such an impression on their dull and uneventful lives, but they were only a small part of the thousands of women who fell in love with him. He was constantly pursued by women

41

at the opposite pole of society. Invitations – to luncheons and dinners, to villas and yachts in the south of France – poured in on him. He was charming and sweet to all, but he was clever enough to evade any entanglements.

What none of the women who tried to engage Ivor's special attention for themselves seemed to realise was what kind of person he really was. The theatre was the one great, all-absorbing love in Ivor's life. His heart, soul, and all his talents belonged to it. He was a very simple and completely natural person, who loved to spend his few leisure hours in his home, surrounded by old friends, talking about the theatre with them or listening to a new record of Kirsten Flagstad singing *Tristan und Isolde* or the *Götterdämmerung.* He would perhaps play a game for a short time, then pick up a book he had not had time to read or a big block of paper and some pencils to jot down any ideas that might come to his mind during the night, then go to bed to read and write until dawn.

It has always fascinated me to observe the difference between the image a celebrated person presents, and the real person. A friend of ours in Hollywood was one of the most beautiful and glamorous stars of the screen and a great sex symbol for millions of men. She received thousands of letters with offers of marriage and promising a life of great wealth and luxury. She married three times, hoping that each of the husbands would understand her as she really was but though she tried to make the marriages work they all ended in the divorce courts.

The trouble was that the men had envisaged married life with her as exciting and exotic. Their disappointment was acute when, after waiting eagerly for her return from the studios, they found that all she wanted was to put on her bedroom slippers, sit on the floor in front of the fire, roast chestnuts, pop corn, and be left in peace.

While Ivor was making the film of *The Rat* he wrote another play called *Downhill* in which Phyllis Monkman acted with him. It had a long run and was made into a film in which he starred. Thrilled and encouraged by the good notices that he and his two plays had received, Ivor began to write a third play, *The Truth Game.* There were two important women's parts in it, and a good comedy role for himself. The play was very topical, centring on a parlour game which was having an enormous vogue at the time. He persuaded the beautiful Lily Elsie, who had created *The Merry Widow* in England, to come back to the stage and play opposite him.

He always had been thrilled by her beauty and glamour, and the day he first met her – at a party given by his friends the Asquith family at 10 Downing Street – was an unforgettable one for him. Elsie, as all her friends called her, became a close friend, and Ivor often accompanied her at the piano when she sang at charity concerts. She had retired from the stage and was living with her husband in their castle in Scotland when Ivor read the script of *The Truth Game* to her.

'He was the only person in the world who could have persuaded me to go back to the theatre,' she told me, 'but it was a lovely part, the play was very amusing, and I knew what fun we'd have acting together.'

The theatre public, who never had forgotten her in *The Merry Widow*, was thrilled to see her on the stage once more and gave her an ovation at every performance. The situations and the dialogue were the cleverest that Ivor had ever written, and the play was a huge success. After a long run in London it toured all the principal cities of Britain.

Ivor followed this with *Symphony in Two Flats* which was equally successful. During the run of *Symphony*, Lee Shubert, one of America's leading producers, visited England and he was so impressed with the play and with Ivor's perforn ance in it that he decided to take it to America with the British cast intact. Ivor was very excited at the chance of starring in one of his own plays in New York where he had never acted before.

He was especially happy that Benita Hume was to be his leading lady, as he considered her one of the most talented young actresses in London. She made a great personal success in *Symphony* and repeated it two years later in Ivor's comedy *Party*. Off-stage, she and Ivor had a private language of their own which no one else could possibly understand and which they loved to use in crowded places where they could say exactly what they wanted without anyone knowing. Benita made a considerable success in films in England and then went to Hollywood where she married Ronald Colman.

2
American Interlude

AMERICAN INTERLUDE

IVOR NOVELLO ARRIVED in New York in the late summer of 1930. He could hardly have come to America at a worse time. The stock market collapse ten months earlier had changed the lives of almost everyone. Fortunes had been wiped out overnight and people who had made a great deal of money during the previous years and had become accustomed to a luxurious way of living now found themselves confronted with a crisis they could not resolve. It was not just gamblers who suffered; many people put up their gilt-edged securities as guarantees in order to hold on to their speculative stocks which had completely collapsed. In the end they were forced to sell out at very low prices and lost also their solid investments.

As always, the first items people had to cut down on were luxuries, and they found that they could not afford to go to the theatre as they had before. Theatre after theatre closed down, and only a few plays which were not expensive to run, and which were either farces or comedies that would make people laugh and forget their problems for a few hours, could survive.

It was impossible to put on new plays because the normal financial backers had no money to invest, but the Shuberts, who had brought Ivor and an English company to New York, owned several theatres which they could not afford to keep closed. No matter how little money came in at the box office, it was better than nothing at all. But with Ivor the Shuberts made two great mistakes. In order to open their theatre as quickly as possible they produced the play early in September when a great heat-wave engulfed America. Nobody wanted to be in the city, far less in a theatre which did not have air-conditioning. Secondly, instead of bringing Ivor's play *The Truth Game,* a gay comedy, they chose *Symphony in Two Flats,* a charming play but a sad one. If only they had waited till the autumn and produced *The Truth Game* they would have had a great success.

46

I had met Ivor at several parties given for him after his arrival in America, but there were always groups of friends around him and I hardly had a chance to exchange any conversation with him. But I did go to the opening night of *Symphony in Two Flats*. The heat all day had been terrific and in the theatre one could hardly breathe. A few minutes after the curtain rose the worst thunderstorm of the year broke out and the crashes of thunder were so loud that it was impossible to hear what the actors were saying on the stage. It was a most unfortunate evening, and although the critics gave the play good reviews and praised Ivor's performance, it did not have a chance of survival. After a short run, the Shuberts took it off and the English company, with the exception of Ivor, sadly returned to London.

Ivor had wanted so much to have a success in New York that he was determined not to give up so easily. As the Shuberts found their theatre dark again he persuaded them to put on *The Truth Game* and to cast a major American star opposite him. They decided to ask Billie Burke if she would consider coming back to the stage. She read the play and realised what a good part Ivor had written. She had known him well for many years, and the idea of co-starring in it delighted her. She was a great favourite in America, not only because of her charm and beauty but for her amusing style of portraying the vague and bewildered American society woman.

The Sunday before the rehearsals were to begin Billie and her husband, Florenz Ziegfeld, the famous impresario, gave one of their big luncheon parties at their magnificent home on the Hudson River, about an hour from New York. Billie's secretary telephoned me to ask if I would bring Ivor and Constance Collier in my car with me. They were both in good form and the drive could not have been more enjoyable.

There were about sixty guests for lunch, most of them well-known personalities in the theatre and films. There were also New York society people and a scattering of wealthy financiers who had been backers of Ziegfeld for many years. I believe it was the last big party they gave in that wonderful home, as Billie planned to stay in New York for the

47

duration of the play and Ziegfeld soon afterwards found himself in a financial crisis which led to bankruptcy. (It must be said, in tribute to Billie, that after the run of *The Truth Game* she summoned up all her courage and decided to make a new career for herself in Hollywood. She made such a success in films that she paid off all of Ziegfeld's liabilities, even though she was not obliged to do so.)

Driving home from the party, Ivor asked me if I would like to go to the rehearsals of *The Truth Game* at the Ethel Barrymore Theatre during the next three weeks. 'Come in any time you want,' he said. 'Stay as long as you can and tell me how you think everything is coming along.'

During the rehearsals I got to know Ivor very well and in the evenings we went with friends either to the theatre or to the Metropolitan Opera where the season was just beginning. A week before the play was due to open he told me he would like to give a big party on the first night and invite all the people who had been so kind to him in New York. He had been living in Bea Lillie's apartment on the East River, while she was staying in his flat in London. When she returned I found a smaller flat for him where he and Lloydie, his secretary, could live for the rest of their stay in New York.

'It will be too small to give the party there,' Ivor said. 'Do you think it would be a good idea to take a private room in a hotel?'

'Absolutely not,' I told him. 'We'll have it at my apartment. The restaurant downstairs arranges everything beautifully.'

'That will be perfect,' he said. 'Let's make out the guest list tonight. I'm going to be terribly busy this next week and it would be wonderful if you could arrange the whole thing for me.'

I lived in the apartment next to my parents at Mayfair House on Park Avenue and Sixty-fifth Street. They had a large apartment and we could open the doors between and have plenty of room for big parties. The only difficulty during those days of Prohibition was to find liquor that it was possible to drink without danger of being poisoned. An Italian friend of mine, Tony Lugano, who owned a speak-easy in West Fiftieth Street, always managed – at fabulous prices – to get me fairly good Scotch

48

whisky which came to him direct from the rum-boats operating off the New Jersey shore. But gin was a big problem! It always came in the same type of Gordon bottles but the people who sold it had filtered out the good gin and substituted something horrible in its place. Thus, like so many of my friends, I decided that it would be safer to make my own. I always had several dozen empty gin bottles stored away so I went to a local chemist and bought some gallons of pure alcohol.

The next thing I did was to take off my clothes and put on my bathing shorts. Then I cleaned the bath tub very carefully with alcohol, which of course there was no need to do as I was going to fill it with alcohol anyway, but it somehow made me feel that I was doing it all in a very antiseptic and professional way. Then I poured the alcohol into the tub, on this occasion filling it up to the top as it was going to be such a large party. I had a small flask of essence of juniper berries and this I added to the tub.

I then took a miniature canoe paddle (I kept it just for this purpose) and stirred very briskly so that the juniper juice would blend with the alcohol. Every once in a while I took a sip with a spoon to test the mixture, and it was so potent I felt as if I was drinking liquid fire. After half an hour of stirring I took a ladle and funnel and poured the liquor into the gin bottles which I corked and lined up on the kitchen shelves. I looked very proudly at the bottles I had just filled, thinking how much they would contribute to the happiness of the evening. After watching me at work, Ivor said that if he wrote a play about Prohibition days in America, he could certainly have a 'gin-making' scene in it.

The opening night was a great success for Billie and Ivor and the critics praised the play highly. It was just the right kind of show for that moment and the audiences roared with laughter all through the play. Thus Ivor was able to turn the failure of his first Broadway play into an enormous success with the second one. (It had a long run and MGM bought it as a vehicle for Robert Montgomery. They paid Ivor a large sum of money for it and gave him a contract to turn it into a film in Hollywood.)

All the omens were right for our first-night party and everyone was in the happy mood of celebrating a success. There were stars, both American and English, in abundance, as well as other celebrities, and the Press described it as 'The Party of the Stars'.

The evening was such a success that Ivor and I decided to give a supper party every Saturday night. On these evenings we would play one or two of the games that were so popular in England at the time. The favourite one was a type of charade in which a team acted out each syllable of a word, and then the word itself, which had to be guessed by the rest of the party. Needless to say, with all that dramatic talent available, the games were brilliant to watch and the parties were so talked about that everyone wanted to be invited. The tone was very informal, and often the stars, when they felt in the mood, would stroll over to the piano and sing or play some of their own songs. I recall Bea Lillie singing some of her most amusing numbers in her own inimitable way, and Libby Holman, the famous torch singer, rendering 'Body and Soul' in her husky voice.

Many other famous artists came to the parties. Clifton Webb, starring in the popular revue *Three's A Crowd,* brought Grace Moore, the beautiful blonde soprano who would soon be triumphing with the Metropolitan Opera. The regulars included three well-known producers – Dwight Deere Wiman, Guthrie McClintic, husband of the great American actress Katharine Cornell, and John Wilson. Isobel Jeans, Viola Tree, Edna Best and her husband Herbert Marshall – as well as Ivor and Bea Lillie – were among the English stars always present.

Last summer, forty years later, when I met Margalo Gillmore, the enchanting American actress, at a party in London, the first thing she said to me was, 'I'll never forget those Saturday night parties at your apartment in New York. What marvellous times we had there, didn't we?'

As the Saturday night parties at my home continued I met many more English actors and actresses who had come over to New York on their way to Hollywood. Everything had changed in the film industry with the arrival of talking pictures. Many of the great silent screen stars found it impossible to carry on because of their voices and diction, and so film producers were engaging theatre stars from London and New York.

A veteran stage actress, Laura Hope Crews who had gone to Hollywood to play in character parts and to coach young film aspirants, came to one of our parties with a friend of hers, Ramon Novarro. During the next weeks I saw a great deal of her, and as she knew everyone important in Hollywood I asked her if she thought I could find something to do there. She came up with an idea immediately. She was going to organise a theatre company and take it on a tour of the large cities on the west coast, casting herself in two of the plays that had made her famous in New York, *The Silver Cord* and *When Ladies Meet.*

'I've booked theatres for the four weeks of August,' she said. 'Why don't you come to California and help me? There are so many details that I can't possibly attend to myself and I must have someone I can trust completely. Come out on the first of July when I'm going to begin auditions.'

I thought this a wonderful idea and Ivor agreed. I had been spending a lot of time backstage at *The Truth Game,* and I learned from what I saw there, but now I could learn a great deal more about the theatre and get some of the experience I wanted so badly. Thus it was settled, and when Ivor left for Hollywood in the late spring. I told him that I would join him there on the 1st of July.

I bought a car and engaged a married couple to go with me as I thought it would be best if I took a house of my own instead of staying at a hotel. I let them drive the car to California, and I went by train, which was the quickest way (airplanes were still considered much too dangerous). When I arrived in Hollywood I went to the Beverly Hills Hotel and telephoned Ivor, who was in Santa Monica at the house that he had rented from the director Edmund Goulding.

'Where are you?' he asked.

'I am at the hotel,' I answered. 'I've taken a room here and tomorrow I'll go out and look for a house.'

'What are you talking about?' he said. 'There's plenty of room here for

51

all of us. I'll send the car for you right away. Give up your room and bring your bags with you. I won't take "No" for an answer.'

Ivor's secretary, Lloyd Williams, who had been a great friend of his since their boyhood days in Wales, picked me up from the hotel and on our way to Santa Monica I began to ask him questions. I wanted to know what had been going on since they had arrived and if Ivor was happy with his work.

'I can't say anything,' he said, 'because he wants to tell you all about it himself when he sees you.'

When we were getting near, he pointed out the house to me: I had never seen anything quite like it before. It looked like a little tower perched on a cliff overhanging the ocean, and seemed so small that I couldn't imagine us all staying there. I was sure that the house had been built by some silent screen star without any taste, and that it must be filled with *art nouveau,* as it certainly belonged to that period.

'It's really quite big,' Lloydie said. 'There are three floors below ground level, and there is a marvellous patio where you can take the sun with nothing but the ocean around you. It's like being on a ship.'

Ivor was very tanned, seemed to be in wonderful form, and began at once to tell me about everything that had happened since he arrived in California. Joan Crawford had come to the station to meet him and had given a dinner party for him that night. She called for him in her car the following Monday when he had to report to the studio, and introduced him to all the important people there as, of course, she was one of Metro-Goldwyn-Mayer's greatest stars. He always remembered those kind gestures of her's which made his first Hollywood days so pleasant and easy for him.

Two scriptwriters had begun to change *The Truth Game* into a film scenario before his arrival, and he said it was absolutely ghastly, but he decided that as they had paid him a fortune for the film rights of the play and were giving him a very large salary to turn it into a film, he must do the best he could and overcome all the difficulties. He disliked most the frequent meetings with the writers and producers, all of whom had

24.
Left: A signed photograph to the author from Beatrice Lillie.

Right: Billie Burke who appeared with Ivor *The Truth Game* in New York.

26.
Above: Richard Rose, the author, who presented many of Ivor Novello's greatest stage successes, photographed in 1931.
Right: The author – forty years on.

7.
bove: Isabel Jeans in *The Man In Possession*, New York,
930.

28.
Left: Heather Thatcher who appeared with Ivor in Hollywood in 1931.

29.
Right: Joan Crawford who introduced Ivor to 'everybody' in Hollywood.

30.
Right: The incomparable Greta Garbo –
Ivor's unexpected Hollywood visitor.

31.
Left: Ruth Chatterton who appeared op-
posite Ivor in the Hollywood film of *Once A
Lady.*

different ideas on what should be kept in the script and what should be changed.

While they were working on the film he was asked to help the studio out and write the dialogue for another film – the famous *Tarzan of the Apes,* which they had just begun making. There were only about a dozen sentences of dialogue in the whole picture and he could hardly believe what he had to write for one of the most important scenes, in which Jane and Tarzan were sitting in a tree with all the apes swinging around them. She was teaching him to talk and she pointed to herself, saying, 'Me Jane' and then pointed to him saying, 'You Tarzan.'

Ivor could never get over the fact that they had sent for him, a writer of English drawing-room comedies, to conjure up a few idiotic words in a jungle picture.

Some people have written that Ivor did not like Hollywood because he was lonely, but this was not true as he had friends constantly around him. When he was not working he might dine with Norma Shearer and her husband Irving Thalberg or with Ronald Colman or Dolores del Rio or Laurence Olivier and his then wife Jill Esmond, who were in Hollywood at the time. He did, however, want to act in a film but the studios were busy finding pictures for their own stars like Clark Gable, Robert Montgomery and Ramon Novarro. He was also impatient to get back to London and act in a play of his own and was depressed because he had to wait ten months before he could leave California.

'How do you like the house?' he asked me. 'Doesn't it look awfully empty and bleak? I was waiting for you to go on a shopping tour and get lots of things to brighten it up a bit.'

He had heard of a wonderful oriental shop in Hollywood where they had a wide selection of beautiful Chinese and Japanese porcelains so we decided to go there next day. When we got to the shop we found there was a sale on. The owner told us that because of the Depression people were not buying these expensive things anymore so he had to liquidate his stock. We bought many Celedon green and yellow lamps, two huge antique jade fish to put over the main fireplace, and a big carved jade clock to go between them. We also chose many rose quartz and jade boxes, vases, and ashtrays, of all sizes. When the owner gave us the bill it was tremendous, despite the sale prices, but Ivor loved the things and he did not care what he had to pay for them. After dinner that night we put all the new acquisitions in their places and were delighted to see how much they added to the atmosphere of our temporary home.

Next day Heather Thatcher arrived from England. Ivor had suggested her for an important part in *The Truth Game* and the studio had sent for her. Filming was still being delayed, so we had many happy days in the sun. Heather, Ivor, Lloydie and I played mah-jongg, which had again regained great popularity in America, for hours, sometimes becoming so engrossed in the game that we had dinner served on trays.

The Hollywood stars usually entertained on Saturday evenings as they did not have to be at the studios early the next morning. We went many times to Ruth Chatterton's, and I think Ivor enjoyed the 'musical evenings' at her Beverly Hills home more than any other parties. She was not only one of the biggest stars in films but she saw herself as the leader of a rather intellectual-artistic group and liked to give little 'salons' to which many famous musicians and writers were invited. I remember one night when she gave a party for the German singer Ernestine Schumann-Heinke, who was famous throughout Europe and America. She sang several songs gloriously, and later Jascha Heifitz, the equally-famous violinist, played for the guests. On another evening José Iturbi, who was one of Ruth's best friends, played the piano superbly.

It always seemed strange to me that when one went to the house of a famous film actress for dinner one never met another there. I am sure they must have known each other as they all appeared at the big film premières and charity parties, but in their own homes they seemed to want to have only their little entourage of friends around them. These were usually the people who worked for and with them in one capacity or another: agents and their wives, cameramen and their families, etc. Each star was fixed in her own orbit, with all her satellites moving around her, and there she intended to remain.

One day, after lunch on the patio, Lilyan Tashman, who was one of the film sirens of the day and the wife of Edmund Lowe, the well-known actor, arrived in her car on the way to her Malibu beach house. She wanted to say 'hello' to Ivor and to introduce him to some friends who were going to spend the weekend with her. One of them was wearing a striped sweater, sailor pants, reefer coat, beret, and dark glasses. It was Greta Garbo. Ivor was thrilled to meet her and they talked together for over an hour. He could speak some Swedish which he had learned while doing propaganda work in Stockholm during the First World War, and knew several film directors there who were friends of hers. She seemed to enjoy the conversation immensely and did not give the slightest impression of being the silent and reserved person who only wanted to be left alone.

Ivor was not able to see her again at that time as she was starting work on a film – *Grand Hotel* – which Eddie Goulding was directing.

This was one of the frustrating things Ivor found about Hollywood: so often when he had a reunion with an old friend, or met someone he wanted to get to know better, the person would have to begin a new film, and therefore vanished, in effect, and there was no chance of seeing them again until it was finished. However, Ivor did meet Garbo again in London. They became great friends and she visited him at Redroofs.

We were in San Francisco when Laura Hope Crews opened in a play there. A wealthy elderly man who gave large sums of money to help finance the local opera company and was a great friend of many actors and actresses, gave a party for Laura on her opening night. He asked about fifty people to supper in his large and very old-fashioned home. It happened that at the same time three other veteran American actresses – Ethel Barrymore, Blanche Bates and Mrs Leslie Carter – were also in San Francisco. Laura invited seven or eight of us to go with her to the party. Included was Ramon Novarro who had come up from Los Angeles for her first night. Our host had invited the three other actresses. As each star arrived she would see the others and embrace them in turn. Compliments were exchanged: 'Laura, you were marvellous tonight' or 'Ethel darling,

60

you look more beautiful than ever.' When these formalities were over, each retired to a corner of the huge room where she arranged herself on a sofa, surrounded by her group of admirers. During the whole evening, the actresses never addressed another word to each other and were completely oblivious of everyone else at the party with the exception of their own little group of followers.

At one point Ramon stood up and told Laura that he was going over to talk to Ethel Barrymore for a moment. Laura grabbed him by the arm and said, 'No darling, don't go now. We're having such fun here. Don't spoil it all.' When finally it was time to leave, the earlier ritual was repeated. Each actress embraced the other and said some sweet words to her, they kissed fervently, and then each departed in her own direction, followed by her fans.

When we got back to Laura's hotel apartment, she opened some bottles of champagne and we began to talk about the evening and roar with laughter. Laura had far too great a sense of humour not to appreciate the whole thing and she told us some amusing stories of the rivalry that had existed between all four of them when they were young actresses around the turn of the century. Each was afraid she wouldn't get the leading part in a new play and the other three were almost ill with jealousy if they heard that the fourth had been given a coveted part. This was not a climate in which friendships could flourish and eventually they all became enemies although they tried not to show it in public.

Ivor spent many evenings finishing the play he was writing, the story of a poverty-stricken Russian prince (an excellent part for himself) who found refuge in the home of a small, modest, Clapham family. This became *I Lived with You,* the first play he put on after returning to London. He was also busy writing two other plays, *Proscenium,* which was a theatrical story with a wonderful part for either Gladys Cooper or Fay Compton (and another excellent one for himself) and *Flies in the Sun,* which he hoped to do with Gladys Cooper or Gertrude Lawrence.

One evening Tallulah Bankhead telephoned to say that she had just arrived in Hollywood to make a film and invited us for dinner the following week. Tallulah and Ivor had been friends in London where she had made a sensational success in Michael Arlen's *The Green Hat* and Noël Coward's *Fallen Angels.* When we arrived at her house we found her in a very over-excited state. It seemed that she had been preparing herself all day for the party and had apparently decided to be in one of her worst moods and to try her utmost to shock everybody. She received us at the top of the staircase in a very scanty costume, threw her arms around all of us, and never stopped talking about herself during the entire evening.

After dinner we went to the sitting-room to play some games, but Tallulah's spirits became higher as the evening wore on and she completely ruined the party. Suddenly, when Ivor got up and said that he had to leave because of an early call at the studio the next morning, she asked, 'Darling, I haven't shocked you, have I?'

'You haven't shocked me at all,' Ivor replied, 'but you've bored me intensely.' And he left.

The next day an enormous box of roses arrived at Ivor's house with a card saying, 'Ivor darling, forgive me for last night. You know that I adore you more than anyone in the world. Talu.'

She was to start filming *Lifeboat* the next week and word had gone round that it was going to be a super-film, but it turned out to be just another mediocre one in which Tallulah's great personality and dramatic ability did not come through well. She despised herself in it and said that she didn't want to make any more pictures.

The following year she returned to the stage in New York in *The Little Foxes,* a great success, in which she gave a brilliant performance. We went to see her one evening in the enormous suite she had taken at the Gotham Hotel where many friends were living with her, as usual. The curtains were always drawn so no sunlight ever entered the rooms. She had completely reversed the hours of day and night. They all arose at four o'clock in the afternoon when breakfast was served to them. At eight in the evening, lunch was brought in, after which they played cards, listened to records, and entertained guests until dinner arrived at two o'clock in the morning.

Tallulah said it was the only way to live. 'Daytime is so boring.' she said. 'It's better to sleep through it and have all one's fun at night.'

We did not see her again until we were back in London. It was a fine early summer and I thought it would be amusing to have a different kind of party after the first night of *Full House* so I hired a boat to take us up and down the Thames by moonlight. It was a little battered but I decorated it and hired a small band to play and a caterer to provide all the food and drinks.

On the day of the opening, Bobbie Andrews said to me, 'Who do you think has arrived in London? Tallulah! Shouldn't you invite her to the party tonight?'

'I don't know what mood she'll be in,' I said, 'and as I've asked a lot of old actors and actresses who are great fun but I know aren't exactly crazy about her, I'll pretend I don't know she has arrived. She doesn't really seem right for this affair.'

I was standing at the bottom of the gang-plank, welcoming everybody as they arrived, and just as the last guest was aboard and we were ready to leave I saw someone running down the pier screaming, 'Wait, wait, don't go without me!'

It was, of course, Tallulah.

She rushed up and flinging her arms around me said, 'Darling, I knew you hadn't heard that I was in London or you would have asked me to the party, so I've come anyway.'

Luckily, she was in her sweetest mood and charming to everyone. She kissed all the old actresses, the musicians, and even the cloakroom girl and the chef, and invited them all to her house for breakfast.

I am sure that the teenagers of today would consider Tallulah and her antics, which everyone thought so wild and daring at the time, very old-fashioned and rather boring, so much has social behaviour changed since those days of the thirties.

But to return to the Hollywood scene, one night we had dinner at the

63

home of another very exotic star, then probably the most famous film actress in Europe. She had an enormous oil painting of herself in the living-room of her beach home and she spent many hours a day admiring it. When we arrived, she led us to the picture and pointed out all the beautiful features of her face and body. When we were seated at the dining-room table and supper was being served, she suddenly took off one of her stockings and slippers and put her bare foot on the table, saying, 'Look at my foot! Epstein told me it was the most beautiful foot in the world. Look at the instep and the ankle, and the toes! Aren't they perfectly beautiful?'

When we all said 'Yes', she moved her foot from the table, and it just missed going into Ivor's tomato soup, but we were prepared for any event in the homes of many of the more capricious film stars who were so much in love with themselves and gradually became used to any kind of odd behaviour.

Ruth Chatterton was preparing to make a new film and there was a leading part in it which she thought Ivor might like to play. She sent him the script to read but he was not enthusiastic about it and didn't think it was right for him. He gave it to me to read and I said, 'I agree with you, but as long as you want to act in a film here, why not do it? It's quite a good part, and after all it can't possibly do you any harm. It'll be fun for you to play opposite her as she's such a marvellous actress.'

He thought about it for several days and then decided to do it. He played the part very well, but it did not really do anything for him at all, as the picture itself – *Once a Lady* – was not a success.

Christmas was now approaching and Ivor had already been in America for sixteen months. In February his contract at Metro-Goldwyn-Mayer would end and he would be able to leave. My parents decided to come to California and spend the holidays with me so they took a bungalow at the Beverly Hills Hotel. They had got to know Ivor well in New York and I was happy that they could renew their friendship with him. One day, before they arrived, Ivor began to discuss with me which of his plays would be the best to do first in London.

64

'If we get back in March,' he said, 'we can go straight to work and put a play on early in April.'

'Why do you say we?' I asked. 'I don't see any possible chance of my being there because there wouldn't be anything for me to do.'

'Of course you are coming,' he said. 'You've been with me since I started writing these plays and you have to see them come to life on the stage. You'll be at all the rehearsals and you can help me in many ways.'

'If only I hadn't lost all that money in the stock market crash, I could have produced the plays with you, and then it would have been perfect, but I don't want to go over and be a drag on you,' I said.

'That's nonsense, you have all the money you need to live on and you'll love being in London with us.'

I worried so much about this that I could think of nothing else. I would have asked my parents for money but they had always helped me so much that I didn't like that idea. After arriving in California, my mother had long talks with Ivor, and he read the three plays to her. I believe that she convinced my father that it would be a great opportunity for me to go to England and help produce the plays with Ivor.

That Christmas night Ivor gave a big party for all the friends who had been so hospitable to him during his stay in Hollywood, and my mother and father were invited. Before the party I went to have Christmas lunch with them at the hotel. When I arrived at their bungalow I gave them their presents and then my mother, who was sitting on a sofa at the far end of the room, told me to come and get the present she had for me. She took an envelope out of her bag and said, 'I know this is what you really want most for Christmas.' I opened the envelope and read the letter. It was from our bank in St Paul and it said that they had transferred to the Chase Bank in London a draft for the amount of money that my mother had requested, and that it was being held there for me. I was overjoyed and threw my arms around her and thanked her with all my heart for being so good and so understanding.

Now, suddenly, all my worries were over. I went back to Ivor's house and dashed up to his room, waving the letter in front of him.

'Now I can go with you to London and produce your plays!' I said.

He was very happy and said, 'Your mother is a darling and I felt sure that she would arrange for you to come to London.'

We only had about a month left before leaving Hollywood. Ivor went to the studio every day where they were finally filming *The Truth Game*. Heather Thatcher went with him, and the producers were very happy with the way she played the comedy part that Viola Tree had played on the stage in New York.

We were in the living-room one Sunday afternoon when a beautiful Alsatian dog walked into the house, went to where Ivor was sitting, and lay down at his feet. He seemed very tired, as if he had run miles. Ivor said to Lloydie, 'Doesn't he look just like my Jim?' We decided to put a notice in the local paper to see if we could trace the owner, but there was no response. One day, two weeks later, a letter came from Ivor's housekeeper at Redroofs telling him that his Jim had died. The day and hour of his death were exactly the same as when the new one had walked into the house. Ivor, who was quite superstitious, decided that the new dog had come to him for some mystic reason that he could not understand, and he insisted on taking him back to London with us.

We spent a week in New York seeing plays we had missed while in California and having supper with friends. Letters arrived from Gladys Cooper and Fay Compton. They were both playing in successes in London and would be busy for at least six months more, so there was no chance of their going into one of Ivor's plays at the moment. They were longing to see him again and to have him read the plays to them. Thus *Proscenium* and *Flies in the Sun* would have to be postponed, as Ivor would not consider anyone else playing in them. He was, however, far too impatient to wait for six months before returning to the stage so he decided to put on *I Lived with You* in the meantime.

Auriol Lee, who had directed many successful comedies in London, and John Van Druten, the playwright, were on the boat that took us back to England and Ivor read the play to them. Then he asked Auriol if she would like to direct it. She found it very clever and amusing and they

66

went over the play many times together. Ivor had learned his long part perfectly and they had decided exactly how each one of his scenes was to be played by the time we arrived in Southampton.

The ocean voyage seemed to have done Ivor a great deal of good. He was quite hungry all the time and didn't seem to light as many cigarettes as usual. He always smoked very strong Turkish cigarettes and as soon as he had finished one he lit another. This went on from the moment he woke until the late hours when he went to sleep and especially when he was writing a play or composing music. All his friends urged him to break the habit, or at least to cut it down a bit, but he never seemed able to do anything about it.

As the days at sea went by he became more and more excited about his return to the stage and he could think and talk of little else. A huge crowd of fans was waiting at the pier to welcome him, plus photographers and journalists – and, of course the dynamic Clara Novello Davies.

3
Vintage Actresses~ and Others

THE FLAT

IVOR LIVED AT No 11 Aldwych above the Strand Theatre. It was within a block of some of the most famous theatres in London: the Gaiety, the Aldwych, the Duchess and – his favourite – Drury Lane. Close at hand were the Adelphi, the Vaudeville and the Savoy. All his friends called it simply 'The Flat', and it was usually the centre of their theatrical gatherings which Ivor always loved to have in his own home.

An inconspicuous street door opened into a small rather depressing office hall, at the end of which was a little old lift that could carry only two people at a time. Inside it, one prayed to one's guardian angel for protection as it began its slow, irregular, jolting ascent. Sometimes it stopped completely for a few seconds, and then, for no reason at all, started on its journey again.

Sir Edward Marsh, a great friend of Ivor's, was once caught in it between floors for five hours: it was a miracle that he ever arrived safe at the top floor.

The flat was completely panelled in light oak which gave it a welcoming air of warmth. There were bookcases from floor to ceiling, and the rows of handsome leather bindings lent an attractive colour to the rooms. There were some lovely old mirrors and fine Impressionist paintings on the walls of the drawing-room, which connected with a second drawing-room in which, on a platform, stood the grand piano at which Ivor spent so many hours.

Ivor told me he had changed the decoration of the flat many times and always had great fun doing it. Once, after making a film in Venice, he re-did the entire flat in Italian furniture, covered in red damask, which he brought back; another time, after filming in Budapest, he decided he would go 'Oriental' in style. All the woodwork was painted black, there were low sofas and chairs covered in purple and red and the rooms were completely mirrored. There were ikons hanging from the ceiling and he said that when he had finished it looked exactly like a Turkish brothel. Then he went through an *art nouveau* period, but after many more

70

changes he settled on a calm and classical background.

When we arrived from the boat-train the flat was filled with flowers, books, records, and all kinds of 'welcome home' presents. The telephone rang constantly. Ivor had planned to spend the evening quietly with his mother there (it was the first time he had seen her since his father's death) but when she left after dinner friends began to pour in to welcome him back.

The first few days after his return were hectic. He rushed from one appointment to another, had long conservations with scene designers and costume makers, and with his lawyers, leading to his signing contracts for the Prince of Wales theatre. He was so happy to be home and to have the people he loved most around him once more – Lily Elsie, Zena Dare, Phyllis Monkman, Dorothy Dickson, Eddie Marsh, Harry Kendall, Maidie Andrews, Keneth Kent and Leslie and Gladys Henson. These, together with Beatrice Lillie, Constance Collier, and Noël Coward, who were all acting in New York at the time, were the people he had known since his youth and with whom he had spent the happiest days of his life, both on and off the stage. Later on Peter Graves became a member of this group

I have not mentioned Bobbie Andrews and Lloyd Williams, as they were part of his 'family', and lived in the flat and at Redroofs with him. He had known both of them for years and they did everything they could to make his life run smoothly and to see that he was not bothered by the many little problems and worries that plague most famous people's lives.

Bobbie had been on the stage since he was five years old and was a fine actor. He was clever and witty – a most amusing companion, whom all Ivor's friends loved to be with. His early life had been difficult. This made him very down-to-earth so he had a valuable steadying effect on Ivor and many times when the latter's enthusiasm and fantasy went a bit too far Bobbie would sprinkle a little cold water on them and bring Ivor back to reality. He took care of Ivor's off-stage life, inviting people for luncheons and dinners, and making all the social engagements. He also succeeded in the difficult task of keeping at a distance the scores of people

71

who were always trying to get into Ivor's life, usually for their own profit.

Lloydie took care of Ivor most of the day. He saw that he was awakened in time to keep his many engagements, ranging from meetings with the directors of Drury Lane to luncheons at the Ivy where he entertained several times a week. Lloydie also was in charge of the staff at the flat and at Redroofs (ten in all) and saw to it that both houses were run to perfection. He went on a score of errands every day, and was the contact man through whom people could send and receive messages that Ivor did not have time to cope with himself. He was in charge of the enormous fan mail which occupied him for several hours a day. A talented musician himself, he often helped Ivor in scoring and arranging his music. Besides all this, he was guardian of the large medicine chest, and when Ivor did not feel too well, he knew exactly which medicine, and how much of it would cure the ailment.

His devotion to Ivor since they had been boys together in Wales was so great that he would have made any sacrifice to please him. He proved this once in Hollywood when Ivor said to him. 'Lloydie, there are some of the best plastic surgeons in the world here. One of them was at the studio today and I made arrangements with him to have your nose changed and made much smaller. He'll be waiting for you at ten o'clock tomorrow morning.'

'But I don't want to have it changed,' said Lloydie pathetically. 'I've had it with me so long that I've got used to it.'

'Nonsense,' said Ivor. 'You've often told me how miserable it has made you all your life and what complexes it has given you. It's not going to hurt a bit and you'll see how happy you'll be when it's all over.'

Bravely Lloydie went to the slaughter, and for the next week we were very anxious about how it would all turn out. When finally it was unbandaged he was delirious with happiness as it was a great improvement and he was delighted with his new profile. It really hadn't come off as well as we had hoped it would, though of course we didn't dampen his enthusiasm by saying so.

72

By the end of the week Ivor could hardly wait to get to Redroofs. He was particularly anxious to show it to me as he had talked so much about it when we were in California. It was about an hour from London, at Littlewick Green, a few miles north of Maidenhead. There was a long white wall at the end of the Green with two cottages where the staff lived. Ivor jumped out of the car, opened the gate, and rushed into the garden, shouting 'Here we are at last! Isn't it the most beautiful place you've ever seen?' The house was long and rambling, built of whitewashed brick topped with a red tiled roof. In front, was an enormous lawn bordered with flowers, and in the grounds were found a tennis court, vegetable garden, fruit trees and a solarium.

The cook, the two maids, and the butler ran out to greet him. Entering the house, one came into a small hall on the right of which was a huge living-room with a fireplace on one side, French windows which led into the garden on the other, and a grand piano and writing desk at either end. All of the furniture was upholstered in a heavy white and off-white material and the curtains and the carpet were also white. From that room, one passed into a smaller living-room with the same décor. On the other side of the hall there was a little reception room which led to a beautiful panelled dining-room. Upstairs were five bedrooms which were decorated in various coloured chintzes or in off-white.

Two women decorators, Sibyl Colefax and Syrie Maugham (wife of the novelist) had launched this white and off-white mode, and they designed many of the most important flats and houses in London. They had a large clientèle of theatre stars and society hostesses and the fashion spread all over the country. It seemed to me that every apartment I went to in London looked the same: it was easy to tell at a glance who had decorated it. It was an attractive and effective way of doing up a home, but it was better in the country than in London where the soot and fog soon turned white to off-white and off-white to dark grey.

Only Dorothy Dickson and Eddie Marsh had come down with us for the weekend, as Ivor wanted to spend most of his time going over the script of *I Lived with You* with Auriol Lee who would be arriving later.

73

Ivor Novello's flat at 11, Aldwych, London.

32.
Left: The Hall.
33.
Below: The Drawing Room and Library.
34.
Bottom: Ivor's piano on which he composed so many of his hits.

35.
Left: Ivor's bedroom.

36.
Right: A corner of the Drawing Room with Ivor's favourite chair in the corner.

37.
Below: Ivor's treasured paper weight which bore his name and the engraved first few bars of his famous song – *We'll Gather Lilacs*.

After tea, he went up to his room and changed quickly into grey flannel slacks, a light woollen shirt, and an old tweed jacket – the clothes he loved to wear when relaxing or working. He wasn't interested in the suits that he had to wear around town and on the stage, and loathed going to the tailors to fit them.

He asked me countless times to pick out ties, scarves, and sweaters for him, both in California and in London when he was busy. He seemed pleased with the things I chose for him: often he liked something I was wearing and I would have it duplicated for him. One day when I called at the flat I had a large box under my arm and he asked me what was in it. I told him I had just bought two woollen robes. He demanded to see them, and he liked them so much that he asked me if he could try them on. At that moment his valet, Albert, came into the room and said, 'Those are just what you need so badly, Mr Ivor – a new robe for the theatre and one for the country.' Ivor then said, 'I like these better than any I've ever seen. Do you think you could get me two exactly like them? I haven't time to go shopping.' I could see how badly he wanted them, so I told him to keep them, as I had lots of free time, and could get other ones for myself. He was delighted, and so was his valet.

'Your teamwork is very good,' I said laughingly, 'but next time I'm going to be very careful what packages I bring up here.'

The rehearsals for *I Lived with You* began at the Prince of Wales theatre, and for the next three weeks we spent most of our time there. Auriol was a wonderful companion with a great sense of humour off-stage but she was a rather strange person in the theatre. She was really a very clever woman, and knew a great deal about her job, but it was a bit disconcerting when she fell asleep three or four times during the day, especially when the actors were waiting for her to direct them. However she always awoke with a start and plunged right into her work again.

During rehearsals she told me that she thought the play was lots of fun, adding, 'Of course, we've got Ivor, who's going to be marvellous. His fans will adore him and that's all that's really necessary. It won't make any difference if the critics like the play or not.' I, of course, did not relay these remarks to Ivor who would not have been very amused by them.

The opening night was very exciting. It was the first time Ivor had appeared on the stage since his long absence in America and he had a great reception, with ten curtain calls. The critics' notices were favourable which made Ivor very happy, as he liked the part better than any other that he had yet written for himself. Ursula Jeans played the leading part opposite him with great charm and sympathy and the play did very well for the first months, but in the summer there was a heat-wave and business began to fall off. It picked up in September, but by then Ivor had decided to end the London run and to take the play on tour, something he had not done for a long time.

He had six weeks to rest before the tour was due to begin in late October but he decided instead to play the lead in another play – *Party,* which he had written before going to America. His intention was to put it on for a special Sunday evening performance for theatre people as it was too short for regular performances. But when the manager of the Strand saw a rehearsal, he liked it so much that he asked Ivor if he couldn't expand it so that he could put it on for a regular run in his theatre.

As the play was about an encounter at an after-theatre party between a famous elderly actress and a young girl who had just made a great first-night success Ivor decided to introduce several guest stars who would give solo numbers and amuse the people at the party. This was an original idea and added an hour to the length of the play. Lilian Braithwaite gave a brilliant impersonation of Mrs Patrick Campbell and Benita Hume of Tallulah Bankhead – two of the best parts Ivor had ever written – and the result was not only a long run but the sale of the film rights to Metro-Goldwyn-Mayer as a vehicle for Joan Crawford.

Ivor enjoyed playing in it, and with so many of his friends on the stage with him he said he felt as if he was giving one of his after-theatre parties in his own flat.

When we arrived in London from America in 1931 we were impressed by the spirit and mood of the English people in contrast to the depression in America. The theatre was booming and it was almost impossible to find a vacant one to produce a play in. A new era seemed to have begun in the theatre. A whole group of interesting new writers had appeared on the scene – John Van Druten, Emlyn Williams, J. B. Priestley, Terence Rattigan, and others. Actors and actresses of great promise were climbing towards stardom – Vivien Leigh, Peggy Ashcroft, Celia Johnson, Kay Hammond, Ursula Jeans, Laurence Olivier, Rex Harrison, Alec Guinness, John Gielgud, and Ralph Richardson headed the 'under thirty' list already giving star performances.

In their leisure moments, the theatrical crowd gathered at the Ivy restaurant, and so many people liked to see their favourite stars off-stage that one had to reserve a table for luncheon many days in advance. It was the same in the evening after the plays were over, when the Savoy Grill was the rendezvous: there the stars mingled with foreign diplomats, politicians and well-known society people.

The audiences in the theatres were at that time notably elegant. The women wore beautiful formal evening gowns and sparkled with jewels, while their male escorts always wore white tie and tails. After the play (and sometimes even after the Savoy Grill) many of them would go on to the Embassy Club or to Quaglino's and dance till the small hours. During the London Season there were many great balls in private homes or in hotels.

I was surprised to see so many Rolls-Royces and Daimlers in the streets, and the shops were full of people buying luxurious and expensive things. It was true that many of the wealthy aristocrats had lost their fortunes during the war and that the younger members of the family had, of necessity, gone to work, but on the other hand there were many new fortunes being made by men whose names where unknown a few years earlier. Foreign trade was at a new peak and the pound sterling was worth over four dollars, which meant much to the prosperity of the country.

I was lucky to have Sir Edward Marsh guide me in my first wanderings around London. As one of Ivor's oldest friends he spent many of his leisure hours at the flat and at Redroofs. He was everything that Americans believed an English gentleman should be – tall, slim, erect and perfectly turned out, and he wore his monocle with a great air of distinction. He was a Victorian in manners and in morals, but his interests were attuned not only to the present but also to the future. He was a highly cultured man and had written a biography of the poet Rupert Brooke as well as other notable books and essays.

He had done what was then called the 'Grand Tour' of Europe with Winston Churchill. Both were lovers of paintings, music and all the other arts, and they spent several memorable months travelling in France, Italy and Greece. Later Eddie became Churchill's private secretary and when eventually, after years of government service, he retired, he was given a knighthood.

Eddie was widely known as a patron of young painters and poets and he dedicated his life to discovering and promoting the talents of these young people who came to him for advice and for an appraisal of their works: he had a very critical eye and would immediately see their merits or defects. When he discovered someone with real talent he did everything in his power to help – finding a gallery in which the unknown artist could hold his first exhibition, writing articles in the newspapers and magazines to bring the newcomer to the attention of the public.

He was himself a great collector: the walls of his flat were hung five rows deep with paintings of his protégés. He persuaded his wealthy and influential friends to begin collecting the works of the new young artists and urged the editors of the literary magazines to publish new poets. In his will he left his art collection to the Tate Gallery.

He was a rather Spartan person to whom the luxuries of life were unimportant; in his home he led a simple and methodical life. He had an old housekeeper who had cared for him since he was a child. When she was over eighty and completely deaf she still did all the housework – the floors and the furniture shone – and when he entertained at luncheon parties she cooked delicious meals and served the guests.

She was a little butter-ball of a person, always dressed in black with a white lace collar. She was loved by all Eddie's friends and some of them have written affectionately about her. When Eddie had had his bath in the morning, he would find all his clothes for the day laid out in his bedroom – tie, shirt and socks of colours that blended best with the suit he was to wear. Neither she nor Eddie had any family, and they had become so close over half a century that they never found it necessary to explain anything to each other.

It was a great experience to go to one of Eddie's luncheons. One always met brilliant and interesting people – Lord and Lady Astor, Bernard Shaw, Clemence Dane, Max Beerbohm, Somerset Maugham and the Duchess of Rutland are just a few of the famous names I recall. In the evening, he was always occupied. He never missed the opening of a new play. If there was no first night he would be at a dinner party or reception in one of the fashionable London houses where his charm and wit always added to the enjoyment of the evening.

He planned his summmer holidays the preceding winter and carefully recorded the dates of his arrivals and departures. He would begin his tour at Cliveden, Lord and Lady Astor's home, and after exactly ten days there he would go to Bullbridge, the house of Lady Juliet Duff near Wilton. From there he would proceed to other stately homes throughout England and Scotland.

He exercised a powerful literary influence upon Ivor whom he met just after the success of *Keep the Home Fires Burning.* Ivor had not gone to university but instead, after leaving school had studied at a musical conservatory in London. Eddie would select the books he thought Ivor should read – usually historical and biographical ones – and tried to impart something of what he had learned during his classical education at Oxford. Ivor rapidly assimilated everything Eddie passed on to him but when Eddie tried to persuade him to enter into the social life of London it was a lost cause. Ivor had occasionally gone to dinners, embassy receptions and charity balls when he was beginning in the theatre; Eddie told him it would be good for his career to be seen at such events, but they bored him, and soon he became far too busy to find the time to attend them.

THE TOUR

IN OCTOBER WE started on a long tour of *I Lived With You*. Opening in Manchester, we went on to the principal cities of England and Scotland. I had seen evidence in New York and in London of Ivor's popularity with all classes of people, but it was not until we arrived in the provincial cities of Britain that I fully realised what a tremendous following he had. The theatres in each city were completely sold out long before we arrived and at every performance the 'House Full' sign had to be put up. Queues for the pit and gallery stretched around the block.

When Ivor came on to the stage the first time the applause lasted at least ten minutes and when the company took the curtain calls at the end of the play the reception was such that Ivor had to make a speech every night.

Then at the stage door hundreds of people waited to see him come out and get into his car. They jammed the street and pushed and struggled to get a better or closer view. It always took several policeman to keep order while the crowd waited for him to appear. There was no controlling them; they pressed around him and many of the girls pulled the buttons off his coat and jacket and tried to throw their arms around him. The screams of 'You're the most wonderful . . .' (or words to that effect) rose to a crescendo. It was amazing, and frankly rather terrifying, to see the frenzy of those girls, and when the car finally drove off poor Ivor was so battered that he didn't know whether to laugh or to cry. But by the time we got back to the hotel he had regained his usual poise and there was always a large supper party for our friends in the company or others who had come up from London to see the play again.

When we visited the resort towns Ivor had a wonderful time. He adored fairgrounds or amusement parks. At Blackpool, for instance, he was as happy as a young boy when he led all the members of the company to the roller-coaster which was a hair-raising one. He bought tickets for three rides for each of us and told the men at the gate not to let any of us out till the rides were over. At the end of the first one I had had enough and I tried to get the starter to let me out of the car, but Ivor yelled, 'Don't get out. We're just beginning. You'll spoil all the fun,' so I grimly fastened my belt again and suffered two more rides. Ivor enjoyed the whole thing so much he had to try every stunt and sideshow – he could only be stopped by the fact that he had to get to the theatre.

Before we returned to London I told Ivor that I was going to buy a car as something had to be done to relieve our transport problems. Being a very generous person, Ivor loved to have his friends around him at all times, and he took so many of them to Redroofs at weekends that the car had to be sent back and forth two or three times.

When he went to a matinée he would tell Bobbie to get six seats or more and took everyone to lunch at the Ivy before going to the theatre. His Rolls-Royce, with room for five people, was totally inadequate, especially as his chauffeur had to wait for him outside the flat during the day to take him at a moment's notice to a conference or a rehearsal, and in the evenings had to remain outside the stage door in case some friends had to be called for and brought back to his dressing-room, or taken to a restaurant where he would meet them after the play. There was also the question of his mother who had to be driven to Redroofs every Friday evening.

Ivor agreed with me that we must have another car immediately, but he thought that he had a much better plan than mine. He had seen the newest Rolls-Royce model in London and had fallen in love with it as it was lighter and smaller than his own and would be much easier to handle in the city. He decided to give it to himself as a Christmas present and give me the one he had been using. He said that this meant that we could take five people in one car, and four in the other, which would be absolutely perfect. He wanted me to take Mam to Redroofs on Friday nights together with friends who wanted an extra day in the country, and then he would come down on Saturday night when the play was over, and bring the rest of the guests with him.

'Isn't this a wonderful arrangement?' he asked, and without waiting for an answer hurried out of the hotel on his way to the theatre. Actually, I did not think it was a good idea, as I wanted to get a smaller car that I could drive myself. The thought of having a chauffeur driving me around in a huge Rolls-Royce seemed far too grand and pretentious for me at twenty-eight years of age. However, as I knew how much Ivor enjoyed making plans for all of us, and how well all these had turned out in the past, I decided it was best to go along with him.

The new car was delivered promptly and soon we were using both cars but even then there did not seem to be enough room for all the people Ivor wanted to have with him. I felt certain that before long we would have to have a third car, which proved to be the case.

The best thing that happened on the tour was that Ivor found time, somehow, to write a new play, *Fresh Fields.* He had had the idea in his head for several weeks after some friends had told him that many aristocratic ladies with long social pedigrees had finally found a way to replenish their dwindling fortunes. They took girls from wealthy families in the United States, Canada and other countries into their homes, giving them *entrée* (and chaperoning them) to the debutante balls and social events of the London Season. The girls would meet 'the right people', in many cases be presented at Court, and the hope was that they would meet nice young men with titles who might want to marry them. Who could tell what wonderful things might happen!

For these services, the girls' parents would willingly pay large sums of money. At first only a few daring Society women had done this, but word spread around quickly, and before long many of them were discreetly indulging in this profitable practice. Private agencies made the contacts and conducted the negotiations. All this seemed to Ivor to have the ingredients for a funny play, and the more he thought about it the more it appealed to him.

One night after the theatre he went to his room and began to write. The characters came to him so clearly, and the amusing situations followed one another so rapidly, that in ten days it was finished. He often said that the play he had written in the shortest time had enjoyed the longest run. When we returned to London he immediately got in touch with Lilian Braithwaite and Ellis Jeffreys, the two veteran comediennes for whom he had written the play. When they read it they were delighted, realising what good parts and amusing lines he had written for them.

Ivor decided to do the play immediately after Christmas at the Criterion theatre, just before he would star with Gladys Cooper in his other play, *Flies in the Sun.* But before that he had to go to Paris for several days to film exteriors for *Sleeping Car.* a picture he was to star in with Madeleine Carroll. It is little wonder that the London newspapers called Ivor the 'busiest young man in England'.

CHRISTMAS

WITH SO MANY plans in hand, Ivor could spare only a few days to relax and enjoy the holiday at Redroofs. It would be his first Christmas at home since his return from America and he began to figure out how many friends he could invite to stay. The day after we got back from Paris we rushed around buying Christmas presents for all the house guests and for the many others who would come down on Christmas Day. We arrived at the house just in time to decorate the tree and arrange the gifts, and when we had finished and were thinking of going upstairs to bed Ivor suddenly said, 'Let's open the presents now, before we go to sleep. It'll be much more fun. I can't wait for mine until tomorrow.'

'That'll spoil everything,' Bobbie Andrews said. 'Christmas presents musn't be opened until Christmas morning.'

But Ivor would have none of this and began to open his packages with his usual terrific enthusiasm and we all followed him and began to open ours. Everyone seemed happy with their presents but when we had finished I saw that Ivor had a rather anxious look on his face and he seemed to be searching for something.

'Where is your present to me?' he asked at last. 'I can't find it.'

I told him I had left it in an envelope on his desk as I didn't want it to get burned or damaged on the tree. Ivor rushed to the desk, tore open the envelope, and shouted, 'I can't believe it! I can't believe it!' Everybody crowded round him, and Mam, who was settled in her chair at the end of the room with all her packages on the floor beside her, called out 'What is it?'

'It's a swimming pool,' Ivor said. 'This is the contract saying they're going to begin to work on it next week, so that it'll be finished when the warm weather comes. Won't that be wonderful?'

While we had been on tour I had kept wondering what I could give Ivor for Christmas that would particularly please him. One day, when I was looking at some photographs we had taken in the homes and gardens of friends in Hollywood, the idea came to me and as soon as I returned to London I made enquiries and finally found near Maidenhead a construction company that would carry out my plans for the pool.

Lloydie had brought down to Redroofs over a hundred Christmas presents and packages that had come to Ivor's flat in London and he had arranged them all on a long table at the end of the living-room. These gifts were from people who had acted with him in his plays and films, and from fans.

'Now we'll open all of these,' he said.

It was then after two o'clock in the morning and Mam, Dorothy Dickson, Isabel Jeans and several other friends were tired and wanted to go to bed. But four or five of us stayed with Ivor and persuaded him to let us open the packages with him so that it wouldn't take too long. After he had opened each one he told us who had sent it and said how nice it was of them to remember him.

'Here are some hand-painted china coffee cups from Bessy Jackson.

85

She's the girl who works in the chemist's shop next to the flat. Here is a picture-frame from Helen Bronson, the little woman who wraps the parcels at Peter Jones. Here's a present from my Rockers. I wonder what they've given me?'

It was a silver pen and pencil set, and he said: 'They shouldn't have spent all that money. They have to work so hard for it.'

The Rockers were four girls who lived in humble circumstances at Golders Green. They had had to stop their schooling very early and go to work to help support their families. They had grown up together and remained great friends, which was lucky because they were so plain and sad-looking that no one had ever noticed them: they had no young men or even a date, but they found strength in each other's company and stuck together to face the formidable world around them.

Then suddenly something happened which took them by surprise and changed the direction of their lives. Every week they went to see a play, and as they had never seen Ivor, but had read in the papers that he was starring in a play that he himself had written, they decided to go to see him in *The Rat* the next Saturday night. They queued for their seats in the gallery from early in the afternoon. When they saw Ivor come on to the stage and heard him speak his first lines . . . I suppose what happened to them can be best described as love at first sight.

When the play was over they went to the corner of the street opposite the stage door to try to catch a glimpse of him when he came out of the theatre. They did not press around him like most of the other girls did, but he noticed them – four rather pathetic figures, rocking from side to side with excitement, and he crossed the street to talk to them. He asked whether they had enjoyed the play but they were so stunned that they could not find a word to say and could only wave at him as he drove off in his car.

From that night they never missed a performance he gave. Whether it rained and they had to huddle under their one umbrella, or whether the fog was so thick that they could barely see each other, they could always be found standing on the corner, rocking gently from side to side as they waited for him. Hence they became known as the Rockers.

They collected scores of his pictures from his plays and films and covered the walls of their rooms with them. Their entire conversation centred on him. At last they had found romance, or a substitute for it, that filled the emptiness of their lives.

*　　*　　*

At five o'clock in the morning we finally finished unwrapping the Christmas presents and Ivor had time for just a few hours' sleep before Gladys Cooper would come from her home in Henley to go over the script and discuss plans for the rehearsals of *Flies in the Sun*, which they wanted to begin immediately after the holiday.

GLADYS COOPER

GLADYS HAD CHOSEN *Flies in the Sun* instead of *Proscenium* because, she said, she was tired of playing sweet and good women and longed to play a wicked one for a change. Gladys and Ivor decided to direct the play themselves at the Playhouse theatre which she had leased for several years. She had directed several of her plays before and, as Ivor knew exactly how he wanted the play to be done, they did not foresee any problems. However, on the third day of rehearsals, he received an urgent telephone call from the head of the film company that had bought *I Lived with You*, who told him that, because of some confusion in the studio's schedule, they would have to begin the film the next day, instead of six weeks later.

There was nothing Ivor could do about it. He had to film every day and come back to the theatre in the evening to help Gladys direct. It was a difficult play to produce, with two complicated scenes on a beach in the south of France. It was a tremendous burden for Gladys to carry alone especially as her own part was a long and difficult one. During the lunch breaks she often told me how apprehensive she was about the way she was directing the play.

'How do you think the rehearsals are going?' she would ask.

'It's taking shape beautifully,' I would reply. 'But the beach scenes *are* very tricky, and it's a terrific job for you to do alone.'

She was already playing her part magnificently, and in the last act, when she tried and failed to seduce the young man who was in love with her daughter, and began to realise for the first time that she had become too old to attract men any more, she gave a deeply moving performance. At the end of the scene she went to the dressing-table, examined her face carefully in the mirror, and gave a shudder of despair. Then, as if defying age, she put on a lot of make-up and a bright red straw hat, and went forth to find a new lover.

The public, however, had seen Gladys and Ivor so many times as lovers in plays and films and had adored them so much in these sentimental roles, that they could not accept them as unpleasant characters who loathed one another. The idea of Gladys Cooper trying to seduce the husbands of her friends was repellent to her fans, and when Ivor, as a drunken and disillusioned ex-film star, shot himself at the end of the second act, it was really more than they could bear.

On the first night, instead of inviting friends to see the play with me, I went alone to various parts of the theatre to hear what people were saying and to see how they were reacting. It took me only a short time to realise that they hated the play and that it could never be a success.

After a few weeks, we thought it best to take it off and forget all about the sad event. I had never seen Ivor in adversity before, and I wondered how he would take this great disappointment. He rose above the whole thing and simply said, 'I'm sure I'll always have to write a romantic part for myself. That's what the audience wants and that's the only way I can have a success.'

Then he never spoke about it again. It had been a bad dream which had completely vanished overnight.

I saw Gladys a great deal during the rehearsals. When I first met her I thought she must be a very cold and unsympathetic person, mainly because of the direct and clipped way she spoke to everyone, but as I

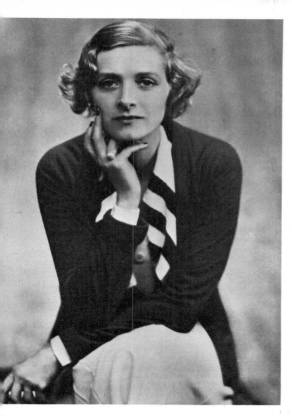

38.
Left: Gladys Cooper.

9.
Right: Ivor with Gladys Cooper
n a scene from the film *Bon-
ie Prince Charlie.*

Two scenes from Ivor Novello's play *Fresh Fields* at the Criterion Theatre, London, 1933.

40.
Above: Lilian Braithwaite, Robert Andrews and Ellis Jeffreys.

41.
Right: Eileen Peel and Robert Andrews in the same play.

42.
Opposite: Lilian Braithwaite, c 1934.

43.
Below: Marie Tempest, who was later to become a Dame, with
Barbara Green in *Moonlight Sonata,* 1937.

gradually began to know her I realised how wrong I had been in forming such a hasty opinion. I found her to be a warm and loyal friend who was so forthright she was incapable of artifice or pettiness of any kind. She loved driving back to her country home after the theatre and her affection for her children, and her desire to spend the days with them there, were the all-important things in her life; acting in the theatre was the only way of making this possible. It seemed to her that the time would never come when she could retire from the theatre and live the kind of life she loved.

One day during the war, when I went to lunch at her home in California, I found her mowing the lawn, and she said with great pride, 'Doesn't the garden look lovely? It's such fun taking care of it, and a great relief from those tiresome days at the studio, but it makes me home-sick for my garden at Henley. I can hardly wait to get back there.'

LILIAN BRAITHWAITE

ATHOLE STEWART WAS busy at the Criterion theatre directing rehearsals of Ivor's *Fresh Fields,* with Lilian Braithwaite and Ellis Jeffreys in the leading roles. It was an inexpensive play to produce as there were only seven people in the cast, and only one set – the drawing-room in the London home of two aristocratic but impoverished sisters. Everything went smoothly during rehearsals and there was an aura of success about it from the beginning. The first night was a tremendous success, with almost continuous laughter and a long ovation and many curtain calls at the end. The critics said it was Ivor's best comedy and it ran for well over a year.

I went every evening to visit the two actresses, and they always had some little complaints, of no importance whatsoever, that they wanted to tell Ivor about. As he was acting in another theatre and could not come to see them, I became a sort of substitute who was to convey to him all

93

the things that were worrying them. They were very jealous of each other, and when they heard me in the corridor one would reach out of her dressing-room and try to pull me in before the other one could. I had to be very diplomatic, a bit of a psychologist and above all, a good listener to them during these often very long sessions.

They were almost exactly the same age, but Lilian wanted everyone to believe that she was by far the younger of the two. Thus she would say very sweetly, and with an angelic expression on her face, 'Poor old Ellis had quite a time remembering her lines tonight,' or 'It's such bad weather for Ellis, I hope the old darling will be able to get home all right.'

Ellis was, in fact perfectly able to remember her lines, and strong enough to get around London at all times.

The question of their ages, however, was not the main thing that bothered Lilian. It was the difference in their salaries. When our business manager asked Lilian about her salary she said that in her last plays she had been receiving eighty pounds a week. This sum was agreed on, and her contract was signed. The next day Ellis's agent announced that she did not attend to any of her financial affairs and left everything in his hands. When he was asked if eighty pounds a week was acceptable he replied that she had received a hundred pounds a week for years and would not consider working for less. He said that she had been a star for many years while Lilian had been only a leading lady. This was not true, but there was no use discussing it further. We had to have Ellis for the part, and her contract was signed. However, Lilian made it her business to find out what had happened and she was very angry; she never forgot that Ellis was being paid more than she was, so there was always a state of tension between them. This amused their friends in the theatre who were always asking how the tug-of-war was going on between the 'old girls' at the Criterion.

Every time I was in Lilian's room the same ritual took place. When she was given a note of the box office receipts for the evening she would put her monocle in her eye, look intently at the figures, and then with a benign smile say to me, 'Lilian has made some more nice pennies for you tonight, Dickie dear.'

Then, of course, I would tell her how much her beautiful performance contributed to the success of the play. This was just what she wanted to hear, and she would say very graciously, 'Ivor's written me a wonderful part and I love to play it. If a part isn't good, no one can make the play successful.'

She was brilliant and witty, and one never had a dull moment in her company. When she was young she had been a beautiful woman, and she still retained a fragile Edwardian loveliness. She was tall, elegant, and aristocratic-looking. *Fresh Fields* was the fourth of Ivor's plays that she had acted in with great success, and he was to write two more big parts for her. He thought her the perfect actress to play the comedy roles in his plays. She knew just how to put a line across and how to extract the maximum laughs from an audience.

The experience of forty years on the stage had perfected her diction and timing. On the subject of diction, she explained to me that if a sentence ended with a consonant she held the consonant for a moment. Thus if the line read 'I'll see you again,' she said, 'I'll see you againnn.' This little trick carried the word clearly to every part of the house. The way she timed the delivery of a sentence was incredible. She was a mistress of the pause. One very warm summer day in the country Ivor was sunbathing in the solarium after a swim in the pool. As he had been told that all the guests had driven over to Henley to see the regatta, he decided to walk around the garden before he dressed, as the sun felt so good on his body. Lilian, however, had not gone with the other guests and had spent the morning relaxing in her bedroom. Then she decided to go into the garden and sit for a while in the shade. As she came out of the house, she opened her large parasol to protect her eyes and her skin, which were very delicate. Suddenly, she spotted Ivor without any clothes on. Undaunted, she scrutinised him carefully from head to toe, and then said, 'What a nice big surprise' – pause – 'to see you up and around so early in the day.'

She was one of the people in the theatre to whom Ivor listened attentively, and when she was enthusiastic about one of his plays he felt it had a great chance of success. She was most amusing off-stage, and her remarks about her fellow artists were so witty, and usually so truthful that they became known as 'Lilians' and were repeated throughout the theatre world. She would deliver them with a cherubic expression on her face, a beguiling smile, and a soft, quivering voice, so that her victims could not be angry, even though there was quite a bitter sting in them.

Once, speaking of another actress, she said, as though puzzled, 'I didn't think she gave such a bad performance, but the audience was very restless and began to leave before the end of the play.' Of a young actress enjoying her first London success, Lilian remarked, 'She's very lovely to look at, but be sure to book your seats in the front rows or you won't hear a word she says.'

The shape of a 'Lilian' was usually the compliment followed by the sting, as when she said of a rival actress, 'She's *good* you know, if one can only forget how frightening she looks with that strange little head on such a tremendous body.' And of a veteran comedienne: 'She's learned all the tricks. The trouble is she doesn't know how to perform them.'

Like Constance Collier and Stella Campbell, Lilian had a great maternal affection for Ivor. They treated him as if he was a young boy long after he had arrived at middle age, and they wanted as much of his attention as he could possibly manage to give them. All three women were superb actresses and brilliant off-stage companions. Lilian was the most conservative and the wisest of the three, while Stella was the most colourful and the most mischievous, and Constance the most ingratiating and the shrewdest. They all had a great impact on Ivor during different periods of his life, because he had the greatest respect for their experience and knowledge of the theatre. They were companions he loved to be with, even though at times they irritated him when they became too difficult and capricious.

Stella and Constance left England to live in America and each of them made only one brief visit to London during the thirties. Stella was living in New York, mainly on her wits and witticisms, while Constance saw a future for herself as a dramatic coach in Hollywood and went there to begin a new career. She became a great friend of the most important film producers who kept her busy teaching the young actresses who were under contract to them. Her greatest opportunity came when Paulette Goddard, the beautiful and popular film star and at the time the wife of Constance's old friend, Charlie Chaplin, asked her to guide and advise her in the films that she was making. They became close friends and Paulette benefited a great deal from Constance's knowledge and experience.

Lilian, however, remained in England and continued her long stage career to become one of the greatest comediennes of the British theatre. She was made a Dame of the British Empire by King George VI. The Braithwaite-Novello combination lasted over ten years, and each realised just how valuable the other was in making his comedies so successful.

MARIE TEMPEST

ANOTHER VETERAN ACTRESS, Marie Tempest, considered herself the first comedienne of the British theatre and few people would have contested her claim as she had given so many delightful comedy performances over a period of forty years. Her public was large and loyal, never missing a new 'Marie Tempest play'.

She was very disciplined, with a strict code of behaviour for herself and those around her, and if they did not adhere to it they found themselves suddenly out of favour, even out of a job. She was a trim little person with a pert and amusing face and she was always perfectly dressed in the latest fashion. She attached great importance to her appearance, and planned her entrances and exits, both on and off the stage, so meticulously that everyone's attention was immediately focused on her.

Although they never went to each other's houses, Marie and Ivor were very fond of each other, and when they met at the Ivy she always embraced him affectionately and insisted that he come to her table for coffee and a little chat. She liked all the young actors and writers and turned on all her charm when she was with them, but she was never enthusiastic about other actresses, especially those of her own age. She did not hold women in great esteem at all and never sought their company, preferring to be with her husband, W. Graham Browne, the actor-director, and their men friends.

She was tolerant though patronising with young actresses when they complimented and paid homage to her, but she became quickly bored and often lost patience with them.

She was the only actress who had turned down a part in one of Ivor's comedies. When she read the script of *The Truth Game*, which her husband was going to direct, she was delighted with the part and seemed happy to co-star with Lily Elsie and Ivor, but during the first rehearsals, when she saw how well the lovely Elsie was playing her scenes, she realised that there was going to be more competition than she had bargained for, and that it would be impossible to walk away with the play, as she was accustomed to doing.

She informed Ivor that the part was not suitable for her, and that she could not attend any more rehearsals. With the opening night only two weeks away, Ivor was in a dilemma and did not know which way to turn. It was during these dark moments that Lilian Braithwaite appeared at the flat and told Ivor that she could not bear to see him in such trouble. She would play the part even though she had not read the script and did not know if it suited her or not. Ivor never forgot this gesture of friendship.

In the theatre Marie Tempest was a complete despot. The director and manager let her have her own way about everything because they knew that otherwise she would create such an inferno that the play could never be put on. At the first rehearsals she would inform the members of the company in no uncertain terms that she was the star of the play which had been written and was being produced solely for her. She would then tell them exactly how they were to play their scenes with her. No one had any chance of sharing the spotlight with her if she could possibly help it.

She treated the poor actors who were to play the parts of the servants as if they were working for her, ordering them to fetch and carry for her during rehearsals.

She held herself very aloof from the young actresses, most of the time ignoring them completely, but she treated the young actors a little better so long as they did not interfere with her lines and her laughs. She was especially fond of Bobbie Andrews, who played her son in several comedies, and always invited him to her dressing-room to have a cup of tea with her between the second and third acts. However, at times he got laughs of his own and that infuriated her so much that she would do anything in her power to bring the audience back to herself. She made funny faces, winked, stuck out her tongue, and once even tore a telephone receiver from the wall and hurled it on the floor so that she would get the audience's attention back. Needless to say, on such days she did not invite Bobbie to her room for tea.

During the thirties she always played the same kind of woman and the plots of her plays were all cut from the same cloth. She would be a wealthy society woman whose children paid no attention to her and did not listen to her advice. But before long they found themselves in trouble, either of a financial or a sexual nature, and in the end they would have to come to her to straighten everything out. Just before the second act curtain came down, she would make a very dramatic speech in which she scolded them for their indiscretions and promised to set everything right if they would let her run their lives in the future.

This speech would always bring an ovation from the audience, and she would respond with many bows and curtsies. As she grew older, she would often forget her lines and substitute those of another of her plays, but as the plots and dénouements were exactly the same in all of them the audience was none the wiser.

One night my parents gave a little supper party for her in their apartment at the Berkeley Hotel. She wore a pink and silver brocade evening dress and a diamond and pearl tiara. Later in the evening my mother told her how lovely she thought the tiara was.

99

'It is sweet, isn't it,' Marie said. 'I inherited it from my great-grand-mother. She had a beautiful voice and was often summoned to Court to sing before the King.'

Walking home from the party, Bobbie Andrews was unusually quiet until at last he said, 'I can't figure out whose Court Marie was talking about. Do you think it could have been Henry the Eighth's?'

When Lilian Braithwaite heard about the tiara the next day she said, 'Great-grandmother fiddlesticks! She bought it last winter at a little jewellers in Wardour Street. He had been trying to sell it to me for years but I didn't think the stones were very good. She would have been much wiser if she had kept her pennies in the bank for her old age, which should be arriving at any moment now. When I was a little girl with my hair in braids she had been acting for many years.'

QUEEN MARY

AFTER THE RUN of *Fresh Fields* had exceeded a year, Lady Carisbrooke, who was a dear friend of ours, telephoned Ivor and told him that Queen Mary wanted to come to see the play the following week and she asked if he could arrange for her to have the royal box. He said he would be delighted to do so.

Lady Carisbrooke was one of the most charming members of the Royal family circle – her husband was the grandson of Queen Victoria and for many years he had lived at Windsor Castle with the Queen, his mother Princess Beatrice, and his sister Victoria Eugenie, who later was to become Queen of Spain.

The Queen was very fond of Lady Carisbrooke and was always prepared to go to any play she recommended. Ivor told me he wanted me to welcome the Queen when she arrived at the theatre, take her to her box, give her his greeting and explain that he could not be there as he was acting in one of his other plays.

'Don't be nervous,' he said. 'She is a darling and puts everyone at ease the minute she meets them'.

He had a great affection and admiration for her and was always happy when she came to see one of his plays. It was also extremely good for the box office because when it became known that Queen Mary had gone to see a certain play many people who followed her every move decided that they must see it too.

On the night she came to see *Fresh Fields* I arrived at the theatre early to make sure all the arrangements had been made. We had ordered masses of roses and lilacs to decorate the front of the box and refreshments were to be brought to her after the second act. I was waiting at the door of the theatre when the black Daimler arrived at exactly a quarter past eight.

When the Queen stepped out of the car she looked so majestic that I was spellbound and could hardly speak the words of greetings that I had memorised. She was wearing a light blue velvet ankle-length cape with a high chinchilla collar, and underneath this was a light blue crêpe dress embroidered in silver with a floral design. She carried a large evening bag of the same colour, and her slippers were also light blue. Her greying hair was beautifully waved in the Edwardian style that she always affected and she wore large pearl earrings and three ropes of enormous pearls around her neck. She also wore rings and a brooch of sapphires and diamonds.

It used to be said that the two finest displays of jewels in the world were to be seen in Cartier's window and on Queen Mary's chest.

I escorted her, with her brother the Earl of Athlone and Lady Carisbrooke to her box and when she entered the audience rose to their feet, turned toward her, and applauded loudly while she bowed and smiled. Then she took her seat at the front of the box and I handed her the programme. She took out her lorgnettes and began to read it very intently. Then she said to her brother, 'Lilian Braithwaite and Ellis Jeffreys. You must remember them. They are wonderful comediennes. I have seen them act since I was a young girl, and they've always been two of my favourites.'

Then she began to ask me questions about Ivor. 'How *does* he do it?' she asked. 'I see he has three plays running at the same time and that he's acting in one of them. He's really quite remarkable. I've followed his career since he wrote *Keep the Home Fires Burning.*'

Then the curtain went up and I left the box to go backstage where I could see unobserved how the Queen was reacting to the play. It was obvious that she was enjoying it tremendously and laughing a great deal. There was a little *double entendre* scene – considered a bit daring in those days – and some of Ivor's friends advised him to take it out that night.*

'Nonsense!' he said. 'It's one of the funniest scenes in the play and she'll love it. I wouldn't dream of taking it out.'

He was right. The Queen laughed through the entire scene and whispered several times to her brother who was also laughing heartily.

At the end of the act, when I returned to the box, the Queen was looking intently through her opera glasses at the audience; whenever she recognised a familiar face she would tell Lady Carisbrooke. I went out to get a box of chocolate-covered mints I had heard that she was very fond of, and when I came back I found her looking intently at my mother, who was sitting in the opposite box with my father and several friends from the American Embassy.

Lady Carisbrooke bent over and whispered something in her ear and the Queen turned to me and said, 'Irene tells me that your mother is in the opposite box. She is beautiful and very elegant. You must be very proud of her.'

'She's wearing the same Molyneux dress that I'm going to wear tomorrow night,' Lady Carisbrooke said.

*The scene in question provides an amusing and interesting example of what was thought *risqué* – or liable to shock Royalty – in the 1930s. Eileen Peel, playing a young Australian girl drops a precious teacup, and it breaks. She is on the floor, trying to stuff the pieces into her bag, when Lilian Braithwaite (one of the two sisters in whose home she is a guest) comes over and, seeing the girl's frightened look, asks her what is the matter. The girl says she is 'in trouble' and is afraid to tell her mother. Lilian assumes the girl means she's pregnant. Sympathetically she asks if she can do anything to help. Yes the girl says, 'you can help me to get rid of it.' Lilian is shocked, but this dialogue of misunderstanding soon resolves itself; as played by Lilian it was very funny indeed.

'Oh that reminds me about yesterday,' said Queen Mary. 'I forgot to tell you that Captain Molyneux came to the palace to fit the wedding dress he's making for Marina. He had just fastened the long train on to the dress when the King came in followed by his new little puppy which promptly ran to the train and settled himself in the middle of it. We were all terrified because we could not coax him off it, and it was impossible to pick him up without stepping on the train ourselves. Finally the King saw a tray of biscuits on a table and he took one and waved it so that the puppy could see it. That solved everything. The puppy ran to him and the King picked him up and carried him out of the room. You can't imagine how relieved we all were, because if anything unpleasant had happened we wouldn't have had the time to send to Paris again for more white satin. I'm sure Captain Molyneux must have been very distressed, but he behaved as if nothing had happened at all.'

After the second act Lilian and Ellis came to the box at the request of the Queen. They floated in wearing the flowered chiffon tea-gowns that they had worn on the stage, curtsied to her, and then settled down to hear all the words of praises that she gave to them. They were like schoolgirls, gazing in rapture at the Queen and treasuring every word she said – which was all highly complimentary to them.

At the end of the play, when the old Australian rancher declares his love to the virginal Lilian who is quivering with terror and joy as he picks her up in his arms and carries her away to marry her, the audience was convulsed with laughter and the Queen could not stop laughing and saying, 'How funny! How terribly funny!' When I saw her into her car she turned to me and said, 'Tell Ivor Novello how much we enjoyed the play and how clever and witty we thought it was.'

As soon as the car had gone I went straight over to Ivor's theatre to tell him all about what had been for me a memorable evening – for which I had him to thank.

Queen Mary had been imbued from childhood with a great sense of responsibility. Once, when a friend asked her if she had wanted to do a certain thing, she replied that she had never thought about what she *wanted* to do, only of what it was her duty to do. People close to her said that she was at heart a timid person, and that she had superimposed on this an air of self-confidence, almost severity, which gave a wrong impression of her real personality.

She was by nature a very inquisitive woman and she was interested not only in the lives of everyone around her but of the people she had read or heard about. She loved every form of art, and in her younger days she has spent many hours studying the paintings in the National and Tate Galleries, learning all about the period furniture in the Wallace Collection, and frequently visiting the treasures in the British Museum. She knew that she was fortunate in being able to have leading art experts to instruct and advise her, and she always remembered everything that they told her.

She was particularly interested in all kinds of *objets d'art* and became a connoisseur and collecter of antique silver, plate, glass, enamels, porcelain, jade, and all kinds of *chinoiserie*. Her collection of jades was one of the finest in the world and she knew the history of each piece. Whenever she had time she would visit the shops and galleries which dealt in these things. A telephone call from the palace would advise the director as to the day and the hour of her planned visit, and he would personally conduct her around the place. He would show her all his acquisitions since her last visit and explain the details of each. She would usually make purchases, either for herself or her family, or to give as presents. She began in January to buy gifts for the next Christmas.

It was a custom for the director to give her a present as a courtesy for her patronage and there was an unspoken protocol about this. She would see something that particularly attracted her, examine it carefully and say how beautiful she thought it was. Then, after her tour was completed, she would stop again to examine the piece that she had admired so much earlier. This was the signal for the director to suggest she should have it, and he would present it to her with a graceful little speech. All this pleased her immensely. She also knew about all the treasures that were to be found in the great homes of England and often when she was making a visit to one of them the family would give her some object of the kind they knew she liked as a memento of her stay there.

Two members of the Royal family were close friends of ours – the Marquess and Marchioness of Milford Haven. He was a great-grandson of Queen Victoria and a second cousin of King George VI. He was also a much-loved man; Ivor regarded him as one of the most charming and sympathetic men in London. He was a great raconteur, and especially interesting when he talked about the years that he had spent at the fabulous Court of Russia with his aunt, the Czarina. The Marchioness – Nada, daughter of the Grand Duke Michael of Russia – was a beautiful and fascinating woman with more *panache* than anyone I have ever known.

She created an aura of glamour wherever she went; I always felt that when one was with her one looked at life through rose-coloured glasses. She never burdened anyone with her troubles, and only a few of her closest friends knew the great strength and courage she had shown when faced with the personal tragedies in her life. Although she had spent her youth in the south of France, her temperament was completely Russian, and she reacted to both joy and sorrow very intensely.

She adored her husband and children, and was happiest when she was at her home in Hollyport, near Maidenhead. Once, when Dorothy Dickson and I were staying there, her son Lord David Mountbatten, and his cousin who was then Prince Philip of Greece, had come home from school for the weekend. When we watched her playing all kinds of games with them in the garden her excitement and intensity made her seem to us to be younger and more enthusiastic than the boys themselves.

When she accompanied Dorothy, Ivor, Michael Duff and myself to France for the World Fair she showed us a completely new Paris that we had never seen before. After the war she and her daughter, Lady Tatiana Mountbatten, went to live near Cannes, where I often visited them, and she always remained brilliant and amusing despite the sorrows she endured.

4
Star-studded
Successes

ZENA DARE

WHEN IVOR HAD written *Proscenium* in California he read it to me and I liked it best of all his plays. There were excellent romantic parts for himself, and for either Fay Compton or Gladys Cooper. There was also a first-class comedy part for a middle-aged woman who would play his mother.

'I've always thought of Zena Dare for this,' he said to me. 'When you meet her you'll realise how perfect she would be in it – so beautiful and elegant. My only worry is that she left the stage years ago and probably won't want to come back.'

Zena Dare and her sister Phyllis began their careers when they were very young and had an adoring public before they were twenty. Their beauty and grace were celebrated not only in England but beyond. There was a craze in the early part of the century for collecting photographs of favourite actors and actresses, and portraits of the Dares were sold by the thousand. Their pictures appeared also on chocolate boxes, playing cards, magazine covers and in shop windows. Horace Wyndham, in his book *Chorus to Coronet,* writes: 'With the possible exception of Mrs Langtry, there can have been few actresses who have been called upon to face the camera more often than Zena Dare. Her photographs have had the place of honour on mantel-pieces in suburban parlours and Belgravia drawing-rooms, in barracks and bungalows from Clapham to Calcutta, from Tooting to Timbuctoo.'

Zena has always said how happy those days were in England. Everyone seemed well off, as there were no taxes to cope with and no sign of the coming war, which was to change the lives of so many Englishmen. It was the day of the 'stage door Johnny'. Crowds of young men from illustrious and wealthy families would come to the stage door to call for their favourite actresses and take them to supper or to a dance. They brought large bouquets of flowers, and tucked inside them were little jewel cases with beautiful rings, brooches or bracelets.

108

'We were all so spoiled,' Zena said. 'We didn't seem to realise how wonderful our lives were.'

It had become the fashion for the most eligible young men in society to marry the famous beauties of the day. Rosie Boote married the Marquess of Headfort; Gertie Millar became the Countess of Dudley; Denise Orme's husbands were Lord Churston and, later, the Duke of Leinster. The Dares were far too busy in the theatre to think of marriage, but one day, the Hon Maurice Brett whose father, Lord Esher, was one of the most distinguished of Edwardian aristocrats, was introduced to Zena. He fell madly in love with her and soon asked her to marry him.

'I'd never thought much about getting engaged,' she told me, 'because I felt I was much too young. But he had such a sweet and funny little face that I couldn't resist him, and we were married soon after. I had been on the stage since I was twelve, and I never wanted to go back to it again.'

When the 1914 war broke out, Gladys Cooper and Zena and Phyllis Dare became the first pin-up girls of the twentieth century. Thousands of young soldiers left for the battlefields of France carrying in their breast pockets pictures of one of these three beautiful women whom they had admired so much in the theatre. Just to take them out and look at them made the agonies of the trenches less unbearable.

As for Zena herself, she accompanied her husband to Paris where he was given an important assignment by the Government. She went to work at Mrs Vanderbilt's American Hospital in Neuilly, where for three years she helped to nurse the wounded soldiers, an experience which she has always remembered with great sadness.

When we returned from America, Ivor talked to her several times about the play, but she always said, 'I'm so happy with Maurice and the children in the country that I can't think of going back to the theatre again. It would be ridiculous at my age.' However, one day about two weeks before rehearsals were due to begin, Ivor telephoned her at Chilston, her beautiful home near Ascot, and said he wanted to come down and read the play to her. She asked us to come for lunch the next day and when we arrived she and her husband and their three children were waiting for us in the garden. The play wasn't discussed during luncheon but afterwards she went with Ivor to a little summer-house where he read it to her. Every once in a while, we could hear her laughing at some lines she thought were particularly amusing. Then they walked around the garden several times, while Ivor explained to her just how he wanted this part to be played.

'You've got to do it,' he said to her. 'You'll be wonderful in it. I haven't thought of anyone else because I wrote it especially for you. The only thing is that you'll have to play my mother, which is ridiculous, as we're about the same age. But I'll be twenty-five in the play, which would mean that you would be about forty-five, and as you look so beautiful and young no one will think about your age. Anyway, forty-five is the most attractive age for women.'

'That doesn't make any difference to me at all,' she said. 'I'd play a woman of eighty if the part was good, and if it wasn't a long one.'

When they came back to the terrace where we were sitting she said to Maurice, 'It's a beautiful play, and it's bound to be a success. Ivor's written a terribly amusing part for me, and, oh dear, I don't know what to do.'

'You're very naughty,' she said to Ivor, 'coming down here where it's so peaceful and I'm so happy, and trying to lure me back to the theatre, which I absolutely hate.'

'You won't be unhappy,' he said. 'We'll all be playing together and you'll be terrific.'

'What shall I do?' she asked, looking at her husband.

'You must play in it, of course,' he replied, 'and we'll all be thrilled to see you on the stage again.'

'Well, I'll do it,' she said. 'When do rehearsals begin? Oh dear, I'm nervous just thinking about it.'

Everything that Ivor had told her came true. On the first night she looked so beautiful and so elegant in the dresses that Edward Molyneux had designed for her and she spoke the witty lines that Ivor had written

110

with such brilliance that the audience gave her an ovation as they welcomed her back to the stage, which she could not leave again until she was over eighty years old.

She played the same kind of chic, amusing, middle-aged society woman in Ivor's *Murder in Mayfair* with equal success, and then she acted at Drury Lane with him in his musicals, *Careless Rapture* and *Perchance to Dream*, and again in his charming operetta – and the last production – *King's Rhapsody*, at the Palace theatre.

She then went to Drury Lane again to play the mother of Professor Higgins in *My Fair Lady*. She never missed a performance in the six-and-a-half years' run, and then went on a long tour of the show through England with equal success.

During all this time I saw her distressed only once, and then just for a few minutes. It was during the first rehearsal of *Murder in Mayfair*, when Leontine Sagan, the clever but rather formidable South African director, was reading the play to the company. When she began the third act, she turned to Zena and said, 'Now Zena, the last act is *completely* in your hands. You won't be the brilliant and witty woman of the first two acts, because the part becomes very dramatic after you hear of your son's suicide.'

Zena looked terrified.

'Ivor, you promised me you'd write only little, amusing parts for me,' she said, 'and now it seems I'm going to be responsible for the entire last act.'

'Don't worry for a moment,' Ivor said. 'You'll be magnificent in it. Just leave it to Madame Sagan and me, and you'll see.'

She must be the only actress in the world who wanted small parts written for her; most of them want theirs to be as long as possible and are always begging the author to give them more lines.

Proscenium was an enormous success. In the prologue, Ivor played the part of an elderly colonel, and in the three acts that followed, he was the colonel's son. It was just the kind of romantic part that he knew how to play so well, and Fay Compton was superb as the ageing star of the theatre, a beautiful and deeply moving performance. The critics praised them both and were enthusiastic about the play.

Ivor and I gave a first night supper party for eighty friends at the Berkeley Hotel. I placed Ivor at the head of the large centre table, and put Fay Compton and Zena Dare, his co-stars on either side of him. Douglas Fairbanks Senior, who was on a visit to London, sat between Fay and Gertrude Lawrence. Sir Edward Marsh was on Zena's left, and Lily Elsie sat on his other side. It was a glamorous party, with most of the celebrities of the English theatre among the guests.

One evening last summer Zena said to me, 'I can't understand why English people are so interested in everyone's age. The older one gets the happier they seem to be. I am quite positive that I was eighty-six on my last birthday, but now the papers say I was eighty-seven. I wish they'd be more careful not to make such horrid mistakes. Oh well, I suppose it doesn't make any difference as long as it makes the public happy.'

LONDON AFTER THE THEATRE

WHEN HIS WORKING schedule wasn't too heavy, Ivor enjoyed going once or twice a week to have supper at the homes of friends after he had finished his performance at the theatre. He particularly liked to go to one of his oldest friends, Adrianne Allen, not only an attractive and talented actress but a most sympathetic person.

She had organised her life so well that she found time to run an antique shop, to do a great deal of decorating, and to write a cook book, in addition to acting. She was extremely popular both in London and New York, and famous for being a wonderful hostess. It made no difference to her whether she entertained ten guests at supper or a hundred at what she jokingly called a soirée. She always invited a congenial mixture of friends and after a perfectly-served supper she would gather everyone in to her beautiful off-white living room to play one of the games she and Ivor were so fond of, particularly the Twenty Questions Game, a version of the old animal-vegetable-mineral game of our childhood days, except that abstract things had been added to those three groups, which made the game much more difficult. The person whose turn it was to choose the subject might, for example, take the last chime at midnight of Big Ben, and then each person would have twenty chances to guess the answer.

There was another enjoyable game where thirty little objects were placed at random on a tray and the guests were allowed to look at them for three minutes only. Then the tray was taken away and the players had to write down a list of articles which they had seen. Also, there were easier games, such as having to name five people, the five books, the five paintings, etc. that one would take along when banished for life to a desert island.

For the last two decades games have gone out of fashion. This would have delighted Ivor's old friend, Constance Collier, who always said that they destroyed the art of conversation, but they will surely come back again, as they always have in the past.

When supper and games were over and the guests were beginning to settle down for gossip and whiskies-and-soda, Ivor would suddenly stand up, say goodnight quickly to everyone, give Adrianne a kiss and a hug, and rush out of the house, to the great surprise of people who did not know him well. This meant that the little group who had come with him had to leave hurriedly also, in order not to miss the ride home in the car. He always explained his hasty departures to us by saying, 'When you feel it's the moment to leave, you should immediately get up and make a quick exit. There is nothing more boring than when people begin to say goodbye, get near the door, and then come back to say something they've forgotten to say before. When a person has done this two or three times his final exit is such an anticlimax that everyone is delighted he has gone at last.'

The only time Ivor went to a night club was when Bea Lillie came to the Café de Paris in London. They had known each other since they first began their careers and had always remained close friends. Ivor was the greatest of all her fans and he always said that her sense of comedy and mimicry was unique in the theatre. 'No one has the star quality and the personality that Bea has,' he said. 'She is the greatest comedian in the world.' Every night when she had finished her act she held a reception in her dressing-room, an international celebrity-party that went on for hours.

Several nights I drove her back to the Savoy Hotel, where she was then staying as she had let her Park Lane apartment when she was playing in New York. One cold, wet night when I was driving home with her she saw some young American sailors sitting on a bench in Trafalgar Square. They had their coat collars turned up and were blowing on their hands to keep them warm.

'Look at those poor little sailor boys,' she said. 'They look frozen and miserable. What a way to spend a night's leave in London.'

She told the chauffer to stop the car, and opening the door, she shouted, 'Boys, come over here. I want to talk to you!'

There were five of them, and they all rushed over to the car.

'What can we do for you, Ma'm?' one of them asked.

'All of you get into the car. We're going home to have some hamburgers and beer,' she said.

They all piled in and when we arrived at the Savoy she took them all up to her suite overlooking the Thames and told them to take off their jackets and make themselves comfortable. She called the night waiter and ordered ten hamburgers, ten hot-dogs, and two dozen bottles of ice-cold beer. The boys were thrilled with Bea's kindness and then one of them, looking at her carefully, said, 'You must be the lady whose picture we saw outside the club. You've got the same little hat on.'

I told him he was right, and that this was the one and only Bea Lillie, whom they must have heard about in America. They were rather overwhelmed by this and became silent until Bea began to play some of her records, which made them roar with laughter and relax.

When dawn came, and they had consumed all the food and drink, they said it was the best night that they had ever had on leave and that they would always remember it. Bea gave them each a signed photograph. When they had gone, she threw herself on the sofa, exhausted. She had given her show twice at the night club, entertained over thirty people afterwards, and then given this impromptu party for the boys. Suddenly, looking like a little girl, she said in a child's voice, 'Baby's tired. Baby wants to go to sleep.' I knocked at her maid's door and said, 'It's very late. Lady Peel wants to go to bed.' Half awake, the woman, who was more a governess than a maid, went to her and said, 'It's time for bed, Milady. It won't be long 'til you have to go to the club again.'

But it was too late! Bea was already fast asleep, and the maid brought pillows and covers to the sofa and tucked her in there.

The annual event that Ivor looked forward to more than any other was the Wagnerian season at Covent Garden. He always took a box for the first cycle of *The Ring* and for *Tristan and Isolde*. The operas were so long that the first act was sung late in the afternoon, then the audiences had dinner either in the Opera House or in one of the restaurants nearby, and returned for the last two acts, which lasted through the evening. This was fortunate for Ivor, as it made it possible for him to hear the first act before going to his theatre and a great part of the last act on his return. When Kirsten Flagstad sang the roles of 'Brunhilde' and 'Isolde', Ivor would sit spellbound by her magnificent voice. She was the greatest Wagnerian soprano of her time, and her glorious singing in the last scenes of *Götterdämmerung* and *Tristan* rose to musical heights unprecedented in the history of opera. Ivor, who later became a great friend of hers, was more thrilled by her voice than he had ever been by any other singer's, and scarcely a day passed either in the flat or in the country without his playing some of her records.

Ivor loved to give supper parties at the flat. He had small gatherings of friends there several times a week, and when any special occasion arose,

115

44.
Overleaf: A scrapbook of 'My Leading Ladies' with inscription by Ivor Novello. The Leading Ladies include Gladys Cooper, Dorothy Dickson, Lilian Braithwaite, Fay Compton, Lily Elsie, Benita Hume, Constance Collier, Dorothy Batley, Madge Titheradge, Phyllis Monkman, Mary Ellis, Vivien Leigh, Isabel Jeans, Zena Dare, Olive Gilbert, Roma Beaumont, Muriel Barron.

my leading ladies

Gladys Cooper
" Enter Kiki! "
" Iris "
" Flies in the Sun "

Benita Hume
" Symphony in Two Flats "
" Party "

Lily Elsie
" The Truth Game "

Lilian Braithwaite
" The Truth Game "
" Symphony in Two
" Party "
" Fresh Fields "
" Full House "
" Comedienne "

Madge Titheradge
" Deburau "
" Proscenium "

Constance Collier
" The Firebrand "

Phyllis Monkman
" Down Hill "
" Sunshine Sisters "

Dorothy Batley
" The Rat "
" Old Heidelberg "

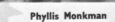

Dorothy Dickson
" Sunshine Sisters "
" Careless Rapture "
" Crest of the Wave "
" Henry the Fifth "

Muriel Barron
" Glamorous Night "
" The Dancing Years "
" Perchance to Dream "

Roma Beaumont
" The Dancing Years "
" Perchance to Dream "

Isabel Jeans
" The Rat "
" The Happy
      Hypocrite "
" Full House "
" Ladies into Action "

Compton
om "
scenium "
der in
   Mayfair "

Zena Dare
" Proscenium "
" Murder in Mayfair "
" Careless Rapture "
" Perchance to Dream "

Olive Gilbert
" Glamorous Night "
" Careless Rapture "
" Crest of the Wave "
" The Dancing Years "
" Arc de Triomphe "
" Perchance to Dream "

llis
rous Night "
ancing Years "
e Triomphe "

Vivien Leigh
" The Happy
      Hypocrite "

Thank you darlings!

45.
Below: Ursula Jeans, 1931.

6.

Below: Noel Coward.

48.
Above left: Dorothy Dickson.

49.
Above: An inscribed photograph of Dorothy Dickson.

50.
Left: The Sunshine Sisters – Dorothy Dickson, Phyllis Monkman and Joan Clarkson, 1933.

51.
Above: Ivor with Phyllis and Zena Dare celebrate the opening
night of *King's Rhapsody*, 1950.

such as the first night of one of his plays, or the visit of some of his good friends from New York or Hollywood, it was an excuse for a large party to which fifty or more friends were invited. His parties became famous. He was a marvellous host, and the evenings were so enjoyable that they went on until dawn, and even later after the first night of a play, as so many of the guests wanted to read the notices of the play in the morning papers before leaving for home.

Ivor never went to the many charity balls to which he was invited, preferring instead to give a special performance of one of his musicals, with the proceeds going to the charity. Once, however, when a group of us arrived for a holiday in Cannes, my mother had some unpleasant news for him. Princess Olga of Greece, the mother of the Duchess of Kent, had heard that he was coming and she asked my mother to persuade him to come to a ball she was giving in aid of poor and orphaned Greek children.

'The sale of the tickets is disappointing,' she said, 'But if Ivor would come we would not have to worry. Everyone would come just to see him.'

Ivor hated the idea but he did not know how he could refuse. If he didn't go, he would be thought unkind, and no doubt Princess Marina, whom Ivor admired so much, would be told he had refused her mother's request. In the end he told the Princess that he would go for just an hour, because he had been working hard all year and needed to rest. She told him that this would be perfect, and that now she would circulate the good news all over the Riviera, which she accomplished in a matter of hours.

When we arrived at the ballroom it was packed with all the hostesses of the Côte d'Azur and their parties, and a great crowd of them converged on Ivor the moment he arrived. He knew most of the English-women, who greeted him enthusiastically and each introduced him to many other guests, until he was completely encircled. At last we made our way to a corner table and Ivor said, 'This is perfectly ghastly. We have to get away as soon as possible.' After a while the lights of the huge room were lowered, the orchestra started to play and the guests began to dance.

'This is our chance,' Ivor said. I pointed to a door that led to the kitchen, and said, 'All right.' We rushed to the door, through the kitchens, and out into the Rue d'Antibes. There was a little film theatre across the street and Ivor said, 'Let's go in. No one will find us there.' The picture was almost over, but we enjoyed what we saw of it, especially as it was *Tarzan of the Apes* which Ivor had made so much fun of when he was working on it in Hollywood.

DOROTHY DICKSON

DOROTHY DICKSON was one of Ivor's dearest friends and he was always happy when she could be with him at the flat or at Redroofs in the country. He was enchanted by her beauty, her personality, and her sense of humour which was as great as his own.

While still in her early twenties Dorothy had become one of the brightest stars of the great American producer, Florenz Ziegfeld, whose *Ziegfeld Follies* were the most lavish and spectacular musical productions in the world. Every year saw a new and even more glorious edition, and he picked the greatest artistes in America to play in them. Fannie Brice, Will Rogers, Eddie Cantor, Grace Moore, John Steele and Ann Pennington were among the stars who shone in his firmament, and he found the most talented songwriters in the country to provide his music and lyrics. His Ziegfeld Girls were famed for their beautiful faces and figures, as well as for the sensational costumes they wore, and they were courted by some of the wealthiest men of America, whom they often married.

One night Ziegfeld was taken to see *Oh Boy,* a popular Jerome Kern musical, in which Dorothy Dickson and her husband and partner, Carl Hyson, were making their stage début on Broadway. He was so captivated by Dorothy's beauty, and by the couple's sensational dancing, that he went to see them after the play and offered them a contract to appear in his new Follies and also on the Ziegfeld Roof where he presented a Midnight Show.

Dorothy and Carl were to become stars overnight, and only a year later they had another big success in the musical comedy *The Royal Vagabond;* on the first night they had to give several encores of their dances.

They decided to have a night club of their own and took over the Palais Royal, a huge establishment on Broadway. They engaged a young bandleader, Paul Whiteman, and his orchestra to play there, and they became famous all over America. The records of Paul Whiteman and his Palais Royal Orchestra were played everywhere and he became one of the greatest orchestra leaders of the day, known as 'The King of Jazz', which was also the name of the film in which he was seen all over the world.

New York Society – 'The 400' – had taken Dorothy and Carl to their hearts, and people who had never deigned to enter a night club before rushed to the Palais Royal and it became the smartest society rendezvous in New York. A table had to be reserved at least a week in advance, and even then it was not likely to be a ringside table as these were continually reserved for important society and financial leaders, European diplomats, and celebrities of the stage and films. By midnight the huge ballroom was full and the noise of music and chatter and popping champagne corks, was deafening. Suddenly, at half past twelve. the lights went out, and silence fell as a great spotlight played on the steps of the silver-crystal staircase, moving to the top step where if focused on the dazzling beauty of Dorothy Dickson. There was great applause as she began to descend – or, as it seemed, float down – the staircase to the dance floor where Carl was waiting to lead her into the first sensational number.

On Saturday nights, when the élite of society had gone to the country for the weekend, the place was taken over by college boys from Yale and Princeton who came in groups of ten or more, lined the walls and hung over the balcony, and caused pandemonium with their chant of 'Dor-o-thy . . . Dor-o-thy . . .' as the time approached for her appearance. When she finally appeared they let out the most tremendous yell and applauded wildly. Many of them stayed on until closing time and then caught the milk train back to college. Being one of them, I was no less enthusiastic, and never missed a Saturday night at the Palais Royal.

When Ziegfeld presented *Sally,* with music by Jerome Kern, he had one of the greatest successes of his lifetime. It was bought for London and Dorothy was chosen to play the star part there. As Sally, the little 'rags-to-riches' Cinderella, she had a triumph on the first night, and the critics gave her wonderful notices. She was so endearing as she sang *Look for the Silver Lining* that she received a standing ovation. She immediately became one of London's most popular musical comedy stars and after the long run of *Sally* she appeared in one musical after another, as well as in many revues.

Ivor was always saying, 'I must write a play for my Dottie. She has more star quality than anyone I know.' At last, he wrote *Sunshine Sisters* for her and for Phyllis Monkman, who was also one of his great friends. With Joan Clarkson, they played three vaudeville sisters who were invited to the country house of a very grand Duchess whose sons had fallen in love with them. There were many neat situations and amusing lines in the play but, although they praised the stars, the critics found it too light and frivolous. It had a nice three months' run, but Ivor was disappointed, and said, 'I made a big mistake. If only I'd set it to music it would have been a great musical comedy.'

Dorothy continued in one success after another. In *Stop Press,* the popular American revue, she was especially ravishing when she sang Irving Berlin's *In Your Easter Bonnet,* in the Easter Parade finale. It was three years before Ivor achieved his ambition to write a star part for her in one of his musicals – *Careless Rapture* – in which she had one of the greatest triumphs of her career.

When *Sunshine Sisters* opened at the Queen's theatre in November 1933, Ivor had three plays running simultaneously in London – the others being *Fresh Fields* at the Criterion and *Proscenium* at the Globe. To celebrate the event, the members of the three companies presented him with a beautiful mirror in the shape of a triptych for his dressing-room table in the theatre, and had all their signatures engraved in the glass.

By now he must have broken a record in the English theatre, as he had had six plays produced since his return from America only a year-and-a-half before. Five had been successes, and only one, *Flies in the Sun*, a failure. Besides acting in two of these plays, Ivor had made three films, *I Lived with You*, *Sleeping Car* and *Autumn Crocus*. He had made a great deal of money in a short time, as he was very highly paid for his film work and in addition to this there were his theatre salary and the royalties from the plays.

He had managed his finances extremely well and was a very good businessman. He listened attentively to all his business manager and the directors of his bank told him, and in the end followed his own instincts which usually proved to be right. He was continually buying annuities, which he found the best way to conserve his fortune. He was also very shrewd about his financial commitments in the theatre and always succeeded in getting the best possible deal for himself and his associates. During all the years that I was producing plays with him I never had to sign a contract of any kind because I knew that he would take meticulous care of every business detail.

Proscenium ran for over eight months to packed houses and Ivor considered it the best of the plays he had yet written. When it ended he felt very tired, which wasn't surprising after the multitude of things he had done in the past year, so he decided he would like to go on a cruise to some warm climate, as the winter in London was especially cold that year. He chose a trip that would take him to Greece, Jerusalem, and Egypt, and he invited Bobbie Andrews, Lloyd Williams and me to go with him.

When we got on the boat at Southampton the Captain had already made many plans. He wanted Ivor to sit at his table, to play the piano at the ship's concert, and to engage in various other social events. Ivor

127

thanked him, but told him he had come on the cruise for a rest and only wanted to be left alone to relax. The Captain understood and passed on Ivor's request so, apart from the fact that when we went in to dinner the first night all the passengers stood up and clapped as he went to his table, he was not worried at all.

Ivor was delighted when he discovered that Clarice Mayne and her niece were sitting a few tables away. She had been a star in musicals for many years, often as Principal Boy in the pantomimes at Christmas. Ivor had known her well for a long time and the two women became part of our little group for the rest of the cruise.

CRUISE

THE FIRST PORT of call was Barcelona, where we spent the morning seeing the sights. At lunchtime Ivor asked the concierge at the hotel if there were any matinées that afternoon. He replied in the negative, but Ivor then looked through the theatre guide himself, and much to his delight discovered that an opera company in a nearby suburb was giving *Madame Butterfly* that afternoon. The concierge was shocked that Ivor wanted to go to see it; the company was a very bad one, he said, and the district where it was playing was the poorest in Barcelona. Ivor insisted and went off by himself to the theatre, leaving the rest of us to continue the tour of the city.

When he came back he told us all about the performance; his description of it was as amusing as the one he had given about *Lohengrin* in his play *Party*. This was his account of the performance: The prima donna was a Spanish lady, nearly six feet tall and weighing at least two hundred and fifty pounds. Just before the curtain went up, the director announced that she had laryngitis and would have to speak her lines instead of singing them. She looked much more like Brunhilde than like Cho-Cho-San, and when she stabbed herself in the last act she fell on the stage so heavily that the floor shook. She must have felt the cold of the theatre intensely because she wore a huge black Spanish shawl over her Japanese kimono, which did not add to the reality of the production.

The tenor was a fragile little man who seemed like a pygmy beside the soprano, and his eyes were so close together that one couldn't have put a pin between them. His voice wasn't too bad, but his grimaces and gestures were so funny that he seemed more like a Mack Sennett movie cop than a United States Naval Commander. Each musician in the six-piece orchestra was out for himself, and they never played in unison. But in spite of all this Ivor had enjoyed his afternoon immensely; he said it proved that even a company as terrible as this one couldn't destroy the music of Puccini. He was surprised to see how deeply moved the audience was. The women around him were dabbing their eyes with their handkerchiefs all through the performance and when Madame Butterfly stabbed herself tears were streaming down their cheeks. 'At the end,' he said, 'there wasn't a dry seat in the house.'

History had always greatly interested Ivor and most of his non-theatrical reading was of historical books. One of the great thrills of this trip for him was to see places and things he had previously only read about. He was deeply moved by the Manger in Bethlehem, the Church of the Holy Sepulchre, the Great Mosque and the Mount of Olives, and it was only on the last day in the Holy Land when, after a great amount of walking and climbing, Clarice sat down on a stone bench and almost crying, said, 'Oh my feet, my poor feet. They'll never be the same again' that we all realised how tirelessly Ivor had led us during those days.

But I think he enjoyed our days in Cairo most. We stayed at the Mena House overlooking the pyramids, and we had an excellent guide, recommended to Ivor by Alfred Lunt and Lynn Fontanne, who had been there the year before. One night the guide organised a picnic supper in the desert, where we were to spend the night. He arranged for tents to

129

be put up and for various entertainments, including a group of young Egyptian galli-galli dancers, with their own orchestra. Ivor and Clarice also got up to perform some impromptu dances of their own, and altogether it was an unforgettable night.

Although Ivor was intensely interested in everything he saw and did, the London theatre was never far from his mind and after a few weeks he began to get restless and wanted to go back to England to work again. He asked me to go to the travel office in Cairo and tell the agents that we were going to leave the cruise at Naples, as he had an urgent call to return to London.

'We'll take the train to Rome,' he said. 'Everyone says the Opera is marvellous since Mussolini arrived on the scene.'

We toured Rome during the day and never missed going to the terrace of the Casina Valadier in the Borghese Gardens to have tea and watch the sun set over Rome. In the evenings we saw wonderful performances of *Aida* and *Turandot,* and Ivor was so happy that he would have prolonged our visit had it not been for his desire to get back to the theatre. The trip had done him a great deal of good. He had relaxed days on the boat and had seen things he would remember for the rest of his life. But now he was ready to go back to the stage again.

HARVEY HOUSE

AFTER WE RETURNED to London Ivor asked me if I would like to invest a little money in some of the plays that Harry Tennent was producing, many of which had been a great success.

'I'll phone Harry,' he said. 'It will be fun and it'll give you an extra interest.'

'You must do it,' Bobbie Andrews said. 'Then we'll know just how well or badly all the plays in London are doing.'

At first I had just a small stake in two plays and both were successes. One was *Call It A Day* by Dodie Smith, starring Fay Compton and Owen Nares, and the other was *Moonlight is Silver* by Clemence Dane, with Gertrude Lawrence and Douglas Fairbanks Junior in the leading roles. Although I had nothing to do with these productions except for my investment, I enjoyed being connected with them even in a small way.

Hugh (Binkie) Beaumont, who was Harry's right hand man and later became the head of H. M. Tennent Ltd, was a friend of mine, and my mother and I went on a trip to Venice and the Dalmation coast with him. When we arrived at the hotel in Venice he opened one of his suitcases and at least twelve play scripts fell on the floor.

'You won't have time to see much if you're going to read all those while we're here,' I said.

'I'll read them each night before I go to sleep,' he replied.

He gave me some of them to read, and the one I liked best was *Harvey House* written by Jane Cowl, one of America's leading actresses. I thought it was just the kind of play that the public liked most. It told the story of three generations of an aristocratic English family and the happy and sad events that happened to them in their London home. It was beautiful, sentimental and dramatic, and I told Binkie that I liked it so much that I wanted to put some money into it. When we returned to London, he gave it to Tyrone Guthrie, one of the theatre's most gifted directors, who was always in demand both in England and in America. There were several other plays that he had been asked to do but he liked this one so much that he said he would direct it before he did any of the others. Fay Compton and Gertrude Lawrence were cast for the star roles and the supporting cast was strong. Everybody connected with the play was wildly enthusiastic about it and rehearsals went along perfectly.

It was a big production with a huge cast and Tyrone was so meticulous with the details of each scene that one became more absorbed in what was taking place in each corner of the stage than in the main plot. At the last dress rehearsal it occurred to me that the stars had become submerged in the trappings of the production.

Harvey House opened at His Majesty's theatre but was not well received by the critics and was so expensive to run that it had to be taken off shortly afterwards. It was the first time that I realised how mistaken the most brilliant and experienced people of the theatre could be. Tyrone Guthrie and all the others connected with the play had felt certain that it would be a great success and they had all been completely wrong. It was a great disappointment to me, and I began to be very sceptical of the theatre as a financial venture. I decided that I had better save my resources for Ivor's plays as they had brought me so much success in the past.

A few years ago Isabel Jeans went with me to see a play at the Vaudeville theatre. Looking at some old play posters which were framed and hanging in the foyer, she said, 'I didn't know you presented *Harvey House.*'

'Neither did I,' I replied. 'They popped it off so quickly that I didn't have time to see a programme.'

I made only one exception to my plan of presenting only Ivor's plays and that was because of completely different circumstances. Sir Michael Duff was a good friend of mine and had been very kind to me when I came to live in London. I had many happy times at his house in London and during weekends at Vaynol, his beautiful home in Wales. He loved the theatre and always wanted to write a play but he felt that he had to have someone with experience to collaborate with him. I introduced him to another friend of mine, Simon Carnes, whom I had met with Hermione Gingold in Budapest. Simon had written some lyrics and revue sketches for her and he wanted to write a play. I suggested that he should go to Vaynol for a while and that he and Michael should try to write a comedy together. They took my advice and when they returned they handed me a hilarious comedy-farce which they called *Back Your Fancy.* I helped to have it produced and we engaged the famous musical comedy star, Alice Delysia, to play the lead. The opening, at the Theatre Royal in Brighton, was a great society event. Lady Juliet Duff, Michael's mother, and Sir Edward Marsh had brought a trainload of celebrities from London and it was a very glamorous first night. The audience laughed and applauded continuously and there were many curtain calls at the end for the artists and for the two young playwrights. The play had a long and successful tour in the provinces but did not come to the West End because it was impossible at that moment to find the right actress for the other star part.

MURDER IN MAYFAIR

WHILE IVOR WAS on a long and very successful tour of *Proscenium* he found time to write a new play, *Murder in Mayfair*. He again wrote excellent parts for Fay Compton and Zena Dare, and a very good one for himself, as a concert pianist, in which he gave one of the best performances of his career. There was a fourth important part which he gave to Edna Best. She made a great success in it as a wicked and disillusioned society girl who is murdered at the end of the second act. The play, produced in 1934, had a long run at the Globe theatre where *Proscenium* had been only a year before.

Ivor believed in the 'star system' and he filled the principal parts in his plays with the most famous actresses he could find. He felt that the more big names there were in a cast the better the chances of success. Even though he was himself a great box office attraction, he always had one, two or three more stars in his companies. If the actress playing opposite him was still too young to have already become famous he made a star of her and put her name up in lights with his; from then on her future was assured.

133

Moreover, he always selected beautiful women to act in his plays. Lily Elsie, Gladys Cooper, Dorothy Dickson and Zena and Phyllis Dare were not only famous for their beauty in England but were among the great beauties of the world.

One Sunday at Redroofs Ivor said to me, 'I must write a new play to act in after *Murder in Mayfair.* I've got an amusing idea about a man, his wife and his mistress, which might make a good comedy.' He then told me the plot of *Ladies in Action* which he produced many years later with Dorothy Dickson and Isabel Jeans as his co-stars.

After luncheon he began to talk about his music as he had many times in the past months.

'I've neglected it for ten years,' he said, 'and it's high time I began again. After I've written this next play I'm going to try to write an operetta.'

Then he went over to the piano and began to improvise as he so often did. After a few minutes he started to play something I had never heard before.

'That's wonderful,' I said. 'Put it down on paper and keep it for that musical you've just been talking about.'

Then suddenly an idea flashed through my mind and I said excitedly, 'Why don't you write a big musical and act in it yourself? You play the straight romantic part and find an actress with a beautiful voice to play opposite you. Let the other actors also sing, and there can be choruses, and ballets in it too. I believe it would be terrific.'

'How did you happen to think of that?' he asked.

'You write good plays and lovely music, and there's no reason why you can't combine the two,' I replied.

From then on he thought of little else and spent many hours every day writing the play and composing the music for a new piece which he called *Glamorous Night.* With his usual generosity he told everyone including his biographer that I had given him a new formula that he used not only for this first musical but for all the others that followed it.

One day, when Ivor was holding an audition for *Murder in Mayfair,*

ove: An autographed *Murder In Mayfair* group – Edna Best,
bbie Andrews, Zena Dare and Fay Compton with Ivor
vello.

3 – 56.
opposite top left: Ivor in *Murder in Mayfair,*
1934, *top right:* Edna Best, *bottom right:*
ay Compton, *bottom left:* Zena Dare, all in
urder In Mayfair.

7.
elow: Ivor and Mary Ellis in *Glamorous*
ight, 1935.

a young poet, whose work had come to the attention of Sir Edward Marsh, arrived at the theatre to see if Ivor could give him a little part in the play. His name was Christopher Hassall and he said that he'd be content to be one of the understudies. He needed work very badly to help him live until the time when, he hoped, his poetry would be acknowledged. He was engaged and some weeks later was sent for by Ivor who had a hunch that this boy might be able to write the lyrics for his songs. He gave Christopher an aria he had written called *Glamorous Night* and asked him to write the lyrics for it as soon as possible. When the young man came back with the words he had written Ivor knew he had found the person he had been searching for to write all the lyrics for *Glamorous Night.* They worked so well together that Christopher went on to write the lyrics for all of the Novello musicals. He was always surprised that Ivor wrote his music so rapidly and had a difficult time keeping up with him. He was also astounded by how happy Ivor was when he was composing.

'Is there anything that is as much fun as this?' Ivor would ask him. 'Don't you adore it?'

A great friendship developed between them during the years that followed and Ivor was for ever calling him at a moment's notice to come to one of the cities he was playing in, or to Redroofs, to write the words for a song he had just composed.

They were alike in many ways. Both had their heads in the clouds while they were working but Ivor also had his feet planted firmly on the ground. Ivor was always pulling Christopher's leg, but fortunately, Christopher had a wonderful sense of humour and didn't mind at all. He discovered that Ivor was fascinated by the lives of the gypsies and their exotic music, and he always pictured him as one of them, especially when he was resting at Redroofs where time meant nothing to him and he simply lived the life he wanted to. Ivor would read in bed till dawn, and then sleep until lunch-time or even later. He observed no formalities and sometimes during dinner would suddenly leave the table, go to the piano in the living-room, and begin to play a song that had just come into his mind. At other times, while playing cards, he would disappear and be found taking a bath.

Like the gypsies he adored the sun and every winter we went on a trip to find it. Those trips proved fruitless until he finally found in Jamaica the warmth he craved. Otherwise Ivor was not an out-of-doors man. He would sometimes take a little walk around the garden to admire the flowers and the fruit trees but would soon return to the house; he was completely uninterested in fresh air or exercise. Whenever any of his friends suggested a walk in the countryside he would ask, 'It's so warm and cosy here, why in the world do you want to go out into the cold?'

5
The Greatest Moment

TO DRURY LANE

A WEEK AFTER we had talked about the musical that Ivor wanted to write, Harry Tennent, the managing director of Drury Lane and a good friend of Ivor's, asked him to lunch at the Ivy. Harry was very depressed as the last productions at the Lane had been failures and the theatre was heavily in the red. They had to have a success now and as there was a lack of big American musicals which were usually well received in the theatre he was at his wits' end to know what to do. Ivor realised that this was his great chance. He told Harry he had written a big musical show and that it was just the thing for Drury Lane. Harry was very surprised at this news and asked Ivor to tell him the plot.

Ivor had been thinking about this for some time and he had conjured up a romantic episode between a young English inventor and a great gypsy prima donna who was the mistress of the king of a mythical Ruritanian country. He now used all his ingenuity to turn this theme into a full-length musical drama, and he told the story so well and with so much enthusiasm that Harry was thrilled with it. He told Ivor that there was going to be a meeting of the directors of Drury Lane the next afternoon and asked him to send the script beforehand so that he could read it to them.

Ivor was daring enough to say that he would even though he knew that he had only twenty-four hours to accomplish this task. He worked during the afternoon and all through the night and had the manuscript of the play completed one hour before the meeting was to begin. Harry read it to the directors who were most enthusiastic about it. They commissioned Ivor to write the music and get the production prepared for an early May opening. From then on Ivor went into complete seclusion, writing the play and composing the music. Only one person, Christopher Hassall, was constantly with him in the studio at Redroofs, where there was a piano, a gramophone, a tape recorder and a machine to make records.

Drury Lane had always enthralled Ivor and he had vivid memories of the productions he had seen there. In 1902, when he was only nine years old, he went for the first time to a matinée there, and after that he never missed a Lane show. As he grew up he studied all the ingredients that were necessary for a success and was confident that he could turn out just the kind of entertainment that the public wanted to see there. He had always been enchanted by gypsies, their costumes, and their lives in the wild plains and mountains of Central Europe, and especially by their haunting music which he had listened to so often when he was filming in Hungary.

He decided that a mythical kingdom, Krasnia, would be the perfect setting for this play. One of the most colourful scenes was a gypsy camp where Mary Ellis and the chorus sang *When the Gypsy Played* which was followed by a spectacular ballet. Militza, the singer, and Anthony Allen, the young Englishman with whom she had fallen in love, were married in gypsy style there to the accompaniment of exciting tzigany music – a scene which always had a magic for audiences.

The entire score was beautiful, and the aria *Glamorous Night,* which Mary Ellis sang magnificently, and the duet *Shine Through My Dreams Tonight,* which she sang with the Welsh tenor, Trefor Jones, remain for me two of the most effective songs Ivor ever wrote.

As usual, he cast the play to perfection. No actress could have excelled Mary Ellis. Her beauty, her dramatic acting and her glorious voice made her performance one of the greatest seen at Drury Lane in this century. Here was 'star quality' indeed – a magnetism that made Militza a vibrant, thrilling person.

Ivor's choice of Barry Jones for the part of the King was exactly right and Leontine Sagan once more proved herself a brilliant and exciting director, the first woman, incidentally, ever to have directed a Drury Lane production.

Ivor did not forget the Drury Lane tradition that the end of the second act had to be a thrilling melodramatic climax, and he provided this with a shipwreck scene which could not have been done in such a spectacular way at any other theatre.

143

The day Ivor presented the Lane's board of directors with his finished script, score and lyrics was one of the red letter days of his career. Oliver Messel, who had designed the beautiful sets and costumes and had gone to the Balkans with Leontine Sagan to select the colourful materials for them, brought a small cardboard theatre with him to the meeting, and as Ivor read the script and the orchestra played the music, he showed each miniature set with puppets, wearing exact replicas of the costumes he had designed. The directors were thrilled with it all and heaped congratulations on Ivor. On their part, they had given him everything he had asked for, including a hundred and fifty actors, singers and dancers and an enormous orchestra. Now they could expect their reward.

Weeks of strenuous rehearsals followed, ending with many full dress ones, as the production was too large and complicated to take on a preliminary tour. It was exciting to watch Ivor. He was everywhere in the theatre. One moment he was on the stage playing a scene with Mary Ellis or the rest of the company and the next moment he was in the orchestra pit going over some passages of his music with the director and telling him just how he had wanted them played. Next he would be in a huddle with Madame Sagan telling her how a certain scene should be interpreted, then he would go to the room where Ralph Reader was arranging the dances and spend long periods listening to the chorus rehearse their songs.

Although he had engaged the most experienced people to direct each part of the production, he was in charge of them all, advising, suggesting, criticising and complimenting them. Everybody listened to him and carried out his wishes because they trusted his judgment and knew what a knowledgeable man of the theatre he was. The stage hands and the carpenters who were building the sets all called him the 'Governor' and had the greatest respect and affection for him. He was putting all of his vitality into this most difficult production, but he was happier than he had ever been before because he saw his play coming to life exactly as he had visualised it.

The dress rehearsals went perfectly and the great night was at hand.

144

Ivor remained outwardly very calm but one could sense the state of excitement he was in, as all the responsibility to the Drury Lane theatre, to the hundreds of people in the production, and to himself, rested on his shoulders.

When 2nd May 1936 finally arrived he was in great spirits as the final dress rehearsal, which had lasted through most of the night, had been a perfect one. He relaxed in the early afternoon by listening to a new album of *Turandot* and at five o'clock he had his usual tea, toast and soft-boiled egg, then went to his bedroom to get an hour's sleep before going to the theatre. On his way to Drury Lane he said that he wanted to appreciate every moment of his evening.

'I'm going to enjoy every minute of it,' he said. 'I've been waiting all my life for this night to come, and now it's here at last.'

As he arrived at the stage door the people in the long queue which had been building up for four days welcomed him with cheers and when he entered the theatre the stage doorman and the stage hands applauded and wished him a great success. There was pandemonium inside the theatre. Western Union boys were rushing in and out, delivering to Ivor's room five thousand telegrams of good wishes for a great success. His dressing-room was filled with so many huge baskets of flowers that they overflowed into the corridor.

William Abbington, the ingenious stage director, Joan Collins and Ralph Reader the dance arrangers, Madame Sagan, the orchestra conductor and several of the principal actors were all awaiting Ivor's arrival so that they could wish him success.

'I've never seen you in an evening dress before,' he said to Madame Sagan. 'You look absolutely beautiful.'

'Well,' she replied, 'I thought I'd better try to look a little glamorous myself tonight.'

While he slowly put on his make-up she had a few last things to discuss with him. No one in the theatre knew the art of *maquillage* as

145

well as Ivor. Gladys Cooper once said. 'Besides all his other talents, he's the best make-up man in the world.'

After he had put on the suit he was to wear in the first scene he walked across to Mary Ellis's dressing-room.

'This is a little first night gift,' he said, as he fastened around her neck a chain of platinum and diamonds from which hung a beautiful cross of rubies.

'Darling Ivor,' she said, and threw her arms around him. 'What a wonderful present!' She loved Ivor very much, possibly more than she would have cared to admit even to herself. 'I'm going to give the best performance of my life for you tonight, darling,' she said. 'I want to make you proud of the glorious music you've written for me to sing.'

When Ivor returned to his room he was glad to be alone. He wanted to think quietly of all that was going on around him It seemed almost impossible to realise that all of the hopes and ambitions of his youth were about to be fulfilled. When he walked on to the stage of his beloved Drury Lane, not only as an actor but also as the author of the play and the composer of the music, all his dreams would have come true. It would be the greatest moment of his life.

While the theatre filled up and the crowd blocking the street outside watched the arrival of the celebrities there seemed to be in the air a feeling of anticipation of a great theatrical occasion.

Backstage, Ivor listened intently as the orchestra began to play the overture; when it had finished and he heard the applause of the audience, he could not stay in his room another minute; he went to the wings before the call-boy came for him. He would be on the stage alone during the first short scene, walking down a little street lined with small suburban houses, carrying his new invention – a kind of television set – under his arm. He had written this scene as a prelude to show the modest background of the hero's life and he had composed a charming and unusual score to accompany it. This scene would provide a contrast to the exciting and glamorous world he was about to enter.

The orchestra began to play this prelude music and he was standing ready to make his entrance. At last the great moment was at hand – the greatest moment of his life! As he walked on to the stage the audience rose to their feet and gave him the most enthusiastic ovation that he had ever received. One of the oldest stage hands in the theatre, who had worked there for forty years, said that he had never heard such applause at Drury Lane. From the start there was no doubt that the audience was thrilled by the play and enchanted by the music. Ivor knew how the public loved the theme of a woman forced to choose between love and duty, especially when the heroine was an actress like Mary Ellis. When, in the end, she renounced her love for the young Englishman, and married the King in the resplendent Cathedral scene, the first-nighters applauded loudly. As for poor Anthony, he returned alone to London and sadly watched the celebrations in Krasnia on his new television invention.

There were so many curtain calls that Ivor had to make a speech. He thanked the audience for their wonderful reception, speaking with such simplicity and humility that the first-nighters gave him another standing ovation.

Glamorous Night completely changed the status of Ivor in the British theatre. He had been the most popular romantic actor, and his clever, witty comedies had always entertained his large public; he had enjoyed long runs, but now, overnight, he found himself one of the greatest stars in the history of Drury Lane. He had made such a personal triumph as a playwright, composer and actor, that he had become one of the most important men in the English theatre.

Ivor came back to the flat one evening during the run of *Glamorous Night* and said that Noël Coward, who had just returned to London, had come immediately to see the play and thought the music was beautiful and Mary Ellis's performance thrilling. Ivor would rather have received praise from Noël than from anyone else in the theatre world. They had first met in Manchester when Noël was a young man trying to get started in the theatre, and Ivor, who was ten years older, had already become a celebrity. They became great friends, and their love and enthusiasm for the theatre were among the many things they had in common.

Ivor always remembered with happiness the night that King George V and Queen Mary came to see *Glamorous Night.* They had the Duke and Duchess of Kent with them in the royal box and they sent word to Ivor and Mary Ellis that they wanted to receive them at the end of the play. When they entered the box King George said, 'We've had a wonderful evening. We enjoyed the play immensely and thought you were both excellent.'

'It's a beautiful operetta,' Queen Mary said. 'I think it's the loveliest music you've written, but we were sorry that the ending was so sad.'

'You made the Queen cry,' the King said to Ivor. 'We wondered if you couldn't change the ending and write a happy one, so that you both meet again and go away happily together.'

'Well, please do try,' Queen Mary said. 'You're so clever it should be easy for you to arrange. That would make it all absolutely perfect and we'll certainly want to see it again.'

When he returned to the flat Ivor said. 'Aren't they marvellous? They're so romantic that they want everything to end happily. Little do they realise that I'd have to rewrite the last scene completely, compose new music for the finale, and begin rehearsals all over again.'

ISABEL JEANS

WHILE HE WAS playing in *Glamorous Night,* Ivor wrote a comedy called *Full House,* which he wanted to follow *Fresh Fields,* whose long run had come to an end. There was a wonderful part in it for Lilian Braithwaite and another for Isabel Jeans, who gave one of her brilliant comedy perfor-mances as a sophisticated society hostess. Heather Thatcher, as a county, horse-loving girl, made up a very amusing trio of stars and the play ran for a year at the Haymarket theatre.

elow: Ivor and Mary Ellis in another scene
om *Galmorous Night*, 1935.

60

Overleaf: The Ballroom Scene from *Glamorous Night*.

61.
Below: Isabel Jeans and Dorothy Hyson, daughter of Dorothy Dickson, in Oscar Wilde's *Lady Windemere's Fan.*

63.
Left: Ivor and Isabel Jeans in Clemence Dane's *The Happy Hypocrite,* His Majesty's Theatre, 1936.

65.
Right: Vivien Leigh.

64.
Below: Ivor and Vivien Leigh in a dramatic scene from *The Happy Hypocrite.*

66.
Left: Dorothy Dickson and Ivor in *Careless Rapture.*

67.
Below: The memorable Rose Ballet from *Careless Rapture* designed by René Hubert.

This was the second of Ivor's comedies in which Isabel Jeans had starred. In *The Rat,* his first play, she had given a stunning portrayal of Zelie, the aristocratic French adventuress with whom Ivor fell in love.

Isabel has always had great style of her own, and her beauty, chic, and elegance are unrivalled in the theatre. When I saw her for the first time, starring in *The Man in Possession,* her performance had the lustrous and exciting quality that I had associated only with those two great actresses, Lynn Fontanne and Gertrude Lawrence. Her intelligence, wit and experience have made each of her portrayals sparkle like a highly-polished gem.

She has had equal success in period plays and in modern ones. She had her first great triumph in the Restoration comedy, *The Country Wife,* and received the highest praise from James Agate, the leading theatre critic of his time. Indeed the critics have acclaimed her one of the finest comediennes on the English stage, which is not surprising when one recalls her Lydia Languish in Sheridan's *The Rivals* and her hilarious Mrs Malaprop in a much later production, although she was far too young and beautiful for the part. She has been superb in Oscar Wilde's comedies and no one can wear costume with the same elegance and panache. When she played Mrs Erlynne in a production of *Lady Windermere's Fan,* and the Duchess of Berwick in another she looked ravishing in the costumes Cecil Beaton designed for her.

Gladys Cooper, who was not given to paying compliments that were not fully deserved, wrote her a letter of congratulation for her brilliant portrayal of Lady Bracknell in *The Importance of Being Earnest.* She was most glamorous as the wicked ex-ballerina in *The Happy Hypocrite.* More recently she gave one of her finest dramatic performances in Jean Anouilh's *Dear Antoine.*

She has also given outstanding performances in films, especially in *Gigi,* in which she played the sparkling, mondaine aunt. The scene in which she gave Gigi a lecture on jewels, and the luncheon scene where she taught her how to eat ortalans, were rare moments of brilliant, high comedy.

In private life, she is an enchanting companion. Ivor loved to have supper at her home in St John's Wood, where she lived with her playwright husband, Gilbert Wakefield. The friendship which began with *The Rat* was enduring. Isabel came to all the gatherings in the flat and spent many weekends at Redroofs. She is still one of the most attractive and fascinating people in any company.

THE HAPPY HYPOCRITE

WINIFRED ASHTON, WHO wrote under the professional name of Clemence Dane, was one of the outstanding writers of her day. In 1935 she gave Ivor the script of a new play she had written, based on Max Beerbohm's fantasy, *The Happy Hypocrite,* and set to music by Richard Adinsell. She thought Ivor would be the perfect actor to play the star part of Lord George Hell, the profligate old rake, whose soul was finally redeemed through love.

In the first act Lord George is sitting with his mistress, a famous ballerina, in a box among the trees of a small open-air theatre when a beautiful girl appears on the stage and does a little dance with her young partner. An arrow sent by Cupid and Mercury, perched on a cloud in the heavens, pierces his heart while he is watching the girl, and falling instantly in love with her he rushes to the stage and tries to embrace her, but the girl, terrified by his ugliness, escapes him and flees to the country.

He goes to a famous London mask-maker and orders a mask of the most handsome man in the world so that he can wear it and win the love of this girl who has so bewitched him. He pursues her to the country and declares his love for her and she, overcome by his beauty and tenderness, goes away with him. They live happily in a little rustic cottage until one day the ex-mistress, with her spies, discovers the hiding-place. She rushes at him and tears off the mask before the trembling girl, but because of his great love, and the redemption of his soul, his own face has become the beautiful one of the mask. Enraged and thwarted the evil ones leave and the couple live happily ever after.

For the part of the girl, Ivor chose Vivien Leigh, who had only once before appeared in the theatre. He had met her one afternoon when he was acting in *Proscenium.* A great friend of his had taken her to see the play and brought her round afterwards to his dressing-room to meet him. 'Vivien is longing to go on the stage,' his friend said. Impressed by her beauty and charm, Ivor suggested she should come on to the stage there and then and play a scene with him. He handed her the script of the act he had just played with Fay Compton.

There was no one near the stage except the assistant stage manager, the stage hands who were changing the sets for the evening performance, and ourselves. Ivor began playing the scene with her, and she read the lines so beautifully and with such emotion and tenderness, that we were enthralled. When she had finished we could not resist clapping our hands with delight,

'You're going to be a great actress,' Ivor said to her. 'I will keep you in my mind and try to write a nice part for you in my next play.' Several years later, when he began to cast *The Happy Hypocrite,* he immediately thought of Vivien Leigh for the part of the girl and he starred her with Isabel Jeans and himself.

We took the play on tour two weeks before opening in London as it was a difficult and complicated production and we wanted it to be in perfect condition before coming to His Majesty's theatre. The audiences in Manchester loved it and we hoped that it would be an artistic success in London even though fantasies had not often appealed to the large theatre public in the past. After the evening performances on the tour a group of us usually had supper in Ivor's hotel suite. Vivien was so enchanting, and had such a wonderful sense of humour, that she and Ivor quickly became great friends and always were happy when they could be together. In Winifred – Clemence Dane – he found another new friend and they were together a great deal during the next years.

James Agate gave the play an enthusiastic review, describing it as one of the most beautiful productions he had seen in years and calling it 'an Easter garland' (it was produced during Holy Week 1936). Other critics were no less complimentary. A 'special' audience, composed of intellectuals, sophisticates and artists (theatrical and otherwise) came to His Majesty's but the play never became popular with the masses and it had only a three months' run.

However, it achieved two important things: it gave Ivor an opportunity to show what a good actor he was in a difficult part, and one that he had not written for himself; and it established Vivien Leigh, who had only been seen before in her first play, *The Mask of Virtue,* as a star actress. A few years later she was an international star after playing Scarlett O'Hara in the film *Gone With the Wind.*

Following this triumph, Vivien gave one superb performance after another, on the stage and in films. She brought to all of them a spiritual and physical beauty that enchanted millions of people. Many critics considered her sensitive and deely moving portrayal of the fragile and ill-fated Blanche du Bois in *A Streetcar Named Desire* the greatest performance of her career.

Off the stage she was an affectionate friend, clever, witty and always great fun to be with. She was a very elegant person, with inherent good taste which was seen not only in her clothes but also in the paintings and antique furniture she collected in her homes. She had the most tremendous *joie de vivre* and after her performance in the theatre she usually went either to a party or gathered together a group of people she loved at her own home where she kept the party in full swing until the early hours of the morning.

She had never been very strong and doctors were always telling her she must take care of her health and live a more quiet and restful life, but she paid no attention to their warnings. She did not seem to care about what might happen to her and continued to use up all the vitality she had. She

160

became gradually weaker until one day she slipped quietly away, an untimely death that was a great blow to the theatre and the film world, and a sad, shocked public mourned the loss of an idol they loved.

CARELESS RAPTURE

WHILE IVOR WAS acting in *Glamorous Night* he wrote another play with music for Drury Lane – *Careless Rapture.* When he presented it to the board of directors they were not as enthusiastic as they had been about *Glamorous Night* and they delayed making a decision. In the meantime Ivor decided to do *The Happy Hypocrite* and to postpone the new musical until the autumn when he would put it on himself if Drury Lane decided not to. However, one afternoon during the run of *The Happy Hypocrite,* Harry Tennent came to see Ivor and told him that the musical running at Drury Lane was not successful, that the directors realised they had been mistaken and now wanted Ivor to produce *Careless Rapture* in the autumn. Ivor agreed, on condition that he had complete freedom to produce the play exactly as he wanted to. He also told Harry that he and his company would put up three-quarters of the capital needed for the venture, which would make him actor-manager and give him the rights he wanted.

Ivor then began to cast the play and to sign up all the people he wanted to have with him in the production. He had written a star part for Dorothy Dickson and had chosen Zena Dare for the kind of brilliant comedy role she knew how to play so well. He signed Leontine Sagan again to direct the play, and the same group of people who had worked with him before at Drury Lane, including most of the singers and dancers.

161

Ivor showed his versatility by choosing a Chinese setting for *Careless Rapture* and by giving his music an oriental flavour instead of the tzygany type of music he had composed for *Glamorous Night*. René Hubert, who had made a name for himself in Hollywood, designed the sets and costumes. Although the play was not as well constructed as *Glamorous Night*, it had plenty of drama, excitement, and comedy in it. Ivor played the roles of two brothers, one good and the other bad. He pursued the bewitching Dorothy from England to China, winning her love in the end.

Apart from the charming comedy scenes together and many dramatic moments which the two stars played to perfection there were several spectacular scenes which were among the best that Ivor had ever conceived. In the first act, a holiday fairground scene on Hampstead Heath, complete with roundabout, always received great applause from the audience. In the second act, there was a magnificent Chinese temple in which Dorothy, as a princess about to be sacrificed to the gods, danced in a beautiful Chinese ballet. Later, in the temple gardens, Dorothy and Ivor fell asleep in the arms of an enormous Buddha and were lifted up to the heavens as Olive Gilbert sang *Why is There Ever Goodbye?*, one of the loveliest melodies that Ivor had ever written.

A spectacular and melodramatic earthquake at the end of the second act was brilliantly directed and the backstage crew used all their ingenuity to bring it about. The scene was a city street in China, lined with two rows of houses. Suddenly the earth trembled and the buildings began to shake and collapse, with bricks and stones flying in all directions as fire and smoke enveloped the entire stage. It was a most realistic and thrilling sight, and the audience gave a sigh of relief when they saw Dorothy, Zena, Ivor and Peter Graves escaping in a carriage.

There was a glorious white-wedding scene at the end of the play. Dorothy was dazzling as the bride and all the company wore beautiful white costumes and stood on a white and silver bridge, awaiting Ivor, who had just escaped from prison and fell exhausted at Dorothy's feet – a sensational finale. The entire score was full of melody and at times it

162

reached the heights of grand opera. There were many critics who believed it was the finest music that Ivor had yet composed.

The curtain calls would have gone on indefinitely had Ivor not made a speech of thanks, taking Dorothy in his arms and kissing her. It was a great night for Dorothy who had never looked more beautiful. She had sung Ivor's music with tenderness and charm, and her dancing had been, as always, breathtaking.

When Ivor entered his dressing-room after the curtain had finally come down his first words were, 'Wasn't Dottie marvellous! She's never sung and danced as well as she did tonight.' It was typical that with all the applause that he, his play, and his music had received, the most exciting thing for him was Dorothy's triumph.

Careless Rapture had a long and successful run. Ivor had triumphed again with his second spectacular production at Drury Lane.

CORONATION BALL

THE TEMPO OF life seemed to be increasing in London all through the 1930s and the climax was reached with the coronation of King George VI in the spring of 1937. Plans for this great event had been made many months before, and during the weeks preceding it the decorations were being put up and the stands were being built along the route of the procession. Members of the royal families of many countries were to be there and every room in the great hotels had been reserved well in advance. Jewels which were only worn on such great occasions as this were being brought out of bank vaults and the famous couturiers of London and Paris were working day and night to complete not only robes for the coronation but gowns for the great ball which was to be held the following night.

When Coronation Week arrived there was a frenzy of excitement. On the great day the streets were crowded at seven o'clock in the morning. The lucky ones had seats in Westminster Abbey or in the scores of stands nearby, while others had access to buildings which lined the route and from whose windows they could watch the procession pass by.

When we left the Berkeley Hotel at eight o'clock the manager told us we were the last guests to leave. We were fortunate enough to have been invited to an apartment in St James's Palace belonging to Sir Piers Legh, an equerry to the King. About a hundred people had assembled there eating sandwiches and drinking coffee while waiting for the 'show' to begin. From one of the windows we saw Queen Mary, magnificently robed, leaving Clarence House to go to Buckingham Palace, where the procession was to form.

Like all royal events in England the whole affair was timed to perfection; at the exact moment that the royal carriages were due to appear at a certain point, they came into sight and passed by. The King and Queen, radiant and happily acknowledging the crowd's cheers, were in the first carriage, while the second carried Queen Mary and the two little princesses. The guards of honour and Household Cavalry were magnificent but one of the most glamorous sights, I thought, was the group of Indian Maharajas in their splendid costumes, riding their Arabian horses as the sun gleamed on their jewelled sabres, held high in the air. It was for them the most exciting event since King George V and Queen Mary were crowned Emperor and Empress of India at the Durbar in Delhi.

On the following night the Coronation Ball was held at the Albert Hall. It was a magnificent spectacle. Ivor had been asked to arrange the pageant, which included a series of historic tableaux, depicting all the Kings and Queens in English history. He himself portrayed King Henry V, Dorothy his French queen, and most of the stars of the English theatre took part. Ivor had been given a box which he had listed in my name as he did not want to attract too many of his fans.

After the pageant many of the stars came to the box and joined our guests. Fortunately the box was a huge one and despite all the coming and going there seemed to be plenty of room for all. The boxes were a dazzling sight, filled with the royalties of Europe, ambassadors of every nation and delegations sent by the President of the United States and the heads of other republics. The most arresting sight, however, was again that of the Maharajas and their ladies in their gorgeous brocade costumes and fabulous jewels.

Ivor and I had a bad moment of anxiety during the evening. The suits of armour we were wearing became so heavy that after the first hours we were unable to endure them any longer and, more important, there seemed to be no way of unfastening them from the waist down. We were in a panic and decided to make a quick return to the flat and get out of the horrible contraptions.

I told the chauffeur to bring the automobile tools up to the apartment and, after trying in vain with icepicks and can-openers, chisels, knives and hammers were used to deliver us at last from our steel prisons. After breathing a sigh of relief we changed into our evening clothes and returned to the ball which was still in full swing. Luckily, no one had even noticed our absence. When we finally left at five o'clock in the morning and the hall was still filled with people, continuously toasting the new King and dancing.

CREST OF THE WAVE

DURING THE RUN of *Careless Rapture* Ivor wrote a new play with music, *Crest of the Wave,* for Drury Lane, which was just as glamorous as the first two musicals had been. Dorothy Dickson was again to star opposite him, and he kept almost all the company of *Careless Rapture* intact.

Christopher Hassall wrote the lyrics once more, Leontine Sagan directed, and René Hubert designed the costumes.

The story was about an impoverished Duke who fell in love with a little film girl and forsook his castle to follow her to Hollywood. There she became a great film star and in the end, after many obstacles, the Duke won her love and they returned to his castle to live happily ever after.

This was a musical comedy, as opposed to *Glamorous Night* and *Careless Rapture,* whose musical scores were of a genre usually associated with operetta. There was a beautiful song, *Rose of England,* sung by a large chorus of armoured knights in front of an old, ruined castle, and a charming melody called *Why isn't it you?,* which Dorothy sang enchantingly. The rest of the music was tuneful and it became very popular, even though it was not Ivor's best effort.

Dorothy, as beautiful as ever, sang and danced her way to another popular triumph, while Ivor played a dual role again. There were several spectacular scenes; in one of them the ruins of a Gothic cathedral took shape and down the central aisle came a procession of the ghosts of the famous men who had prayed there. In another scene, an ocean liner was transformed in a moment into a fully-fledged battleship and the great melodramatic second act finale was a train wreck. One saw the passengers looking out of the windows of an express train racing through the night, and then there was an explosion and only fire and smoke were left on the stage.

Crest of the Wave opened on 1st September 1937 and ran for over a year to record audiences. This musical gave Ivor his third consecutive success – a feat no one had ever achieved before.

low: Ivor in the name role and Dorothy Dickson as
tharine of France in Shakespeare's *Henry V,* Drury Lane
eatre, 1938.

HENRY V

DURING THE LONG run of *Crest of the Wave* Ivor was thinking about what he should do next. He finally decided not to write a fourth musical just then but to make a total change by producing Shakespeare's *King Henry V,* playing the title role himself. The theatre world was astonished at the news. They had never dreamed of Ivor playing in a Shakespearian tragedy and they did not know that he had wanted to do this all his life. He had only once been given the chance – in a scene at a charity performance of *Romeo and Juliet.*

As he had given Drury Lane three great musical successes, the directors were prepared to go along with him, but as there had not been a Shakespearian production there in twenty years they were not very optimistic about the idea.

Ivor, however, was not a person to be influenced by anyone when he had made up his mind about what he wanted to do. He was convinced that he could be a success in *Henry V.* Lewis Casson directed an attractive and colourful production and the principal theatre critics hailed Ivor's performance as 'shining', 'dazzling' and 'deeply moving'.

He had now proved himself to be as fine an actor as he was a playwright and composer. Dorothy Dickson, in her first classical role, was a beautiful and charming Princess Katharine of France. An American friend of ours said that she had made the leap from Ziegfeld to Shakespeare with the greatest of ease. He did not know, however, that on the way she had made a great success in Barrie's *Peter Pan* and in Somerset Maugham's *Our Betters,* thus proving what a versatile actress she was.

Henry V drew enormous crowds to Drury Lane. Everyone wanted to see Ivor play in Shakespeare in the magnificent production that the critics had praised so highly. It looked as if it would have a long and successful run, but in its third week came the Munich crisis with war seeming inevitable. The theatres, including Drury Lane, closed down. Like other buildings of national importance, Drury Lane was sand-bagged to protect it from the ravages of war. Ivor, with great sorrow, put up the final notice which meant that five hundred people would lose their jobs. It was a sad finale to his Shakespearian venture and it seemed to him that the end of the world was at hand. It was a terrible moment for me too. If the war came, I would have to return to America and leave Ivor and all our friends for whom I had formed such a great affection. It would mean that the work in the theatre, which I loved so much, and the way of life that had made me so happy, would be ended indefinitely, and perhaps forever.

Those terrible days before Chamberlain left for Munich will never be forgotten by the millions of people who lived through them. Everyone believed that if war began the Nazis would launch a massive bombing on London. That was the 'blitz' technique. There was so much to do and so little time to do it. The air seemed charged with tension and gloom as more and more people appeared in uniform and anti-aircraft guns were placed in strategic positions.

My parents, who had gone to the American Embassy to find out what plans they should make if war began, were advised to book a passage immediately on the Queen Mary, which was the last ocean liner to leave England before the crisis week. They were told that Americans and other foreigners would only be an extra burden for the English to cope with and that all the Americans in England had been told to leave for home immediately. When they decided to take this advice my mother went to say goodbye to Ivor and to tell him that I must leave with them; she asked him to do everything in his power to persuade me to return to America, even though I was determined not to do so. Thus, under the pressure from my parents and Ivor, I had no alternative; I found myself making quick farewell calls to the friends whom I loved so much and finally arrived at the boat train only a few minutes before it was to leave.

The skies were dark and a great pall of fog enveloped the platform from which the train was to depart. Groups of people were saying goodbye to their loved ones who were leaving for America. There was a terrible silence. Everyone was speaking in whispers, tense and stunned by what was happening.

169

The Queen Mary had the largest list of passengers in its history and most of the travellers had to share their cabins with strangers. The corridors were lined with huge iron cases containing gold, jewels, paintings and other priceless art objects which were being sent to the United States for safe-keeping. Many of these cases had Indian inscriptions on them; they contained treasures of the Indian rulers who thought this their last chance of saving them.

As soon as the ship left France where more people and more crates had been taken aboard, the restaurant was opened and although the tables were all filled, one could have heard a pin drop. The people were silent, anxious and exhausted by the strain they had been going through. When they had to speak they did so in hushed voices and with as few words as possible. Everyone retired to their cabins as soon as dinner had been served and the big salons were dark and no music was played. The fear was that the coastal waters had been mined and that German submarines might be lurking nearby, waiting to destroy this treasure ship.

The night passed quietly and early in the morning children appeared on the decks to play in the sunshine. They laughed and sang as they gathered in groups to try the new deck games they had never played before. All children are blessed with a divine spark that helps them to forget sadness and to grasp every happy moment that comes their way. When their parents saw how well their children were behaving, they became imbued with a new strength and a hope that everything would come out well in the end.

Two days later, when news came that Chamberlain had returned successfully to London bringing the assurance of 'peace in our time', the passengers went wild with joy and the celebrations went on until we arrived in New York. Most of the passengers decided to sail back to England on the return trip of the Queen Mary. I would have been happy too if I could have gone back to London immediately, but family affairs made this impossible.

In March 1939 I arrived in London again, just a month before Ivor's musical *The Dancing Years*, which the critics hailed as his best work and which was to have a ten-year run in London and on tour, was produced at Drury Lane. It was his fourth play in this great theatre and the directors had asked him to make it a simpler production because of the uncertainties of the time. However, even though there were fewer spectacular scenes, the sets and costumes were beautiful and the story was so dramatic, topical and poignant that it thrilled the audiences and became the most popular of all his musicals. It was the greatest success in the London theatre and the biggest hit of the war. People went to see it countless times, soldiers and sailors, home on leave, and reunited with their families packed the theatre at every performance.

The story of the happy and carefree Vienna at the beginning of the century, when the air was filled with music and romance and people were singing and dancing to the beautiful waltzes of the day, appealed to all audiences; and then there was the topicality of the Nazi invasion of Austria many years later, which left the country broken and ruined.

Ivor played the part of a young composer, and Mary Ellis, repeating her success in *Glamorous Night*, was again an opera singer in love with him. A new discovery of Ivor's, Roma Beaumont, made a great success as a young girl who had worshipped Ivor since her childhood days. The music was beautiful and one of the most popular numbers was *The Leap Year Waltz*, which Roma sang and danced with charm and grace. Mary Ellis had two wonderful songs – *Waltz of My Heart* and *I Can Give you the Starlight*, which Ivor had written especially for her, and she sang them magnificently.

It seemed that this show would run for years at Drury Lane and that Ivor's popularity would be greater than ever. But black clouds were gathering too rapidly, and after a series of crises England found herself at war on 3rd September 1939. All theatres and cinemas were ordered to close. The blackout had begun and Drury Lane, sand-bagged once more, became the headquarters of ENSA, the purpose of which was to provide entertainment for troops stationed all over England, and later on the Continent.

The outbreak of the war and the closing of his greatest success left Ivor in deep depression, and even though his days were filled with giving concerts for the troops and entertaining them all over the country, his great hope was to take *The Dancing Years* on a grand tour of England, with the original company and the full Drury Lane production.

At last, a year after the war had begun, he and his friend, the impresario Tom Arnold, took *The Dancing Years* on just such a great tour, which lasted more than eighteen months and which played to capacity audiences everywhere. Thus began a ten-year run of this great success; after the tour *The Dancing Years* returned to London, where the theatres had re-opened with performances beginning at earlier hours in order to cope with the blackout and the bombing.

The Dancing Years was another great milestone in Ivor's life, and his popularity reached the highest point of his career. The scene in which he played the piano, while Mary Ellis sang, and the one in which he went down to the Drury Lane orchestra pit and conducted the orchestra himself, were greeted with great applause. On many occasions during those ten years he left the cast for periods of rest or war work, but always returned to it with new vitality and enthusiasm. With *The Dancing Years* he had become the number one box office attraction of the theatre in England.

6
Enchanted Music

KING'S RHAPSODY

WHEN I RETURNED to Europe from America in 1946 I settled down in Rome as my health did not permit me to spend the long winters in London where I really longed to be again. I was having a very pleasant life despite the fact that most Romans seemed to think that a person over forty was already very old and that there was little left in life for him.

This seemed very depressing to me and though I tried to rise above it certain things continually brought it back to my consciousness. As I went to bed late and didn't arise until noon I had never seen the early morning hotel maid. One day I heard her describing the people on my floor to a new maid.

'They put all the old and sick ones up here,' she said. 'In twenty-seven there's an elderly man with heart trouble and they say he can't last long. In thirty-two there's an old woman with a broken leg and she has to be carried into the lift when she goes downstairs. As for the one in thirty-four which was the number of my room), he must be in a very bad condition because I've never even seen him come out of the room.'

One summer day I put on a new suit that had just come from my Italian tailor and as I was about to go to the street I caught sight of myself in the mirror. I thought I looked pretty well for my age, and rather dashing. I walked down the street to the barber shop and when I entered I saw that all the seats were occupied by people waiting their turn. Suddenly a woman turned to her little son who was sitting next to her and said, 'Get up, Giovanni, and let the old gentleman have your seat.'

This remark depressed me so much that I thanked the woman for her kindness and hurried out of the shop. Another time, when I was riding in a taxi, something went wrong with the engine. 'I have to get the car to a garage,' the driver said. 'I'll call another taxi for you.' When it arrived he shouted to the other driver, 'Can you help me get this old man from my taxi into yours? He's in pretty bad shape and can't make it on his own.'

Needless to say, these constant reminders that one was getting old were very dampening to the spirit, especially as I was only forty-three.

One day in the spring of 1950 I received a letter from Ivor which said, 'As soon as the warm weather arrives you must come back to London to see us and to see *King's Rhapsody,* which everyone thinks is the best thing I have ever done. Be sure to make your plans and let me know as soon as possible the date of your arrival. We'll all be angry if you don't come.'

Angry was a strange word for Ivor to use. During all the years that I knew him I only saw him angry twice and on both of those occasions the anger was caused by some remark that had been made about a friend of his. His loyalty to those closest to him was so great that he would not tolerate even the slightest criticism of them. One day someone told him that a member of his company had said some disagreeable and untrue things about the leading lady who happened to be one of Ivor's favourite friends. At first he did not believe what he had been told and said it was just some nasty theatre gossip, but when it was proved to be true he hastily called the guilty person and told him to come immediately to the flat, where he gave him the worst 'telling off' anyone had ever had.

When the young actor went out of Ivor's flat an hour later he was pale and trembling and tears were pouring down his face. He was sure that he would lose his job and, even worse, that his career would be ruined. He did not know Ivor very well, because he was not asked to leave the company and nothing more was said about the matter. Ivor knew that the lecture he had given the boy would never be forgotten by him and that there was no need of any further punishment.

The second time I saw Ivor angry was when we were in Hollywood. One evening I drove to the studio to call for him, as the chauffeur was ill, and I prepared myself for a long wait because at film conferences time was of no consequence. However, a few moments after I arrived Ivor came rushing out of the studio. He was in a terrible state and for a few minutes he was so angry that he could not speak.

'What is the trouble?' I asked. 'What happened?'

'It's those idiots,' he said. 'They're so busy with all their dreadful films that they don't even want to know anything about the theatre where most of the good actors have had their training.'

It seemed that Ivor had that morning taken to the studio a picture of Gladys Cooper which he had just received from England. Before the conference began he went into the office of the appropriate executive and showed him the picture.

'Oh boy,' said the executive. 'What a beauty she is. Why don't you get her to come over here and we'll give her some tests and see what we can do with her.'

Ivor was furious. Almost shouting, he said, 'That happens to be Gladys Cooper, one of the greatest actresses on the English stage. She has her own theatre and Maugham writes plays for her.'

The film mogul did not seem impressed at all.

'We'll get her out here in the end,' he said. 'Eventually, they all come to us. They have to. The temptation is too great.'

It was at this point that Ivor rushed out of the studio. However, his anger did not last very long. After a few minutes he said to me, 'Let's stop at the Asia Bazaar on our way home and see if those Chinese materials have arrived.'

Gladys Cooper always loved to tell this story, and added, 'You see the film man was right. In the end they did get me out to Hollywood. I couldn't resist the temptation of earning all that money.'

But to return to Ivor's letter which reached me in Rome. I was thrilled at the idea of going to London after having been away for such a long time, but I was terrified too, as the war had changed the way of life everywhere so completely that I feared it might have changed all of us as well. Perhaps life in London with Ivor and his friends would not bring me the great happiness I had known before. It might be better to keep the memories I cherished so much rather than risk the chance that our lives would no longer be compatible and that it would be difficult for us to bridge the years that we had been apart. Ivor himself had been through much personal trouble, especially over the death of his mother, whom he had adored. Also he had been seriously ill with pneumonia. I couldn't help wondering if, despite the continuing success of his plays and his music, he might not be changed.

I had last seen him in 1939 just after the opening of *The Dancing Years.* During its long run he had written three straight plays, and two musicals – *Arc de Triomphe* and *Perchance to Dream.* The first of these, in which Mary Ellis starred, did not receive the usual praise that the critics had always bestowed on Novello musicals. The fact that Ivor was not acting in it himself, as he was still playing in *The Dancing Years,* and its unhappy story of a young artist killed in the war (so that there could be no romance in the second half of the play) dampened the enthusiasm of the theatre public. There was, however, some of the finest music that Ivor had ever composed, in a scene from an opera called *St Joan,* which was performed within the play itself. This Mary Ellis sang superbly and it presaged the operas we hoped Ivor would write some day.

Arc de Triomphe opened at the Phoenix theatre in November 1943 and ran for two hundred performances, being closed when the buzz bombs began their reign of terror on London.

Ivor also decided to end the fantastic run – nearly a thousand performances – of *The Dancing Years* at the Adelphi. Shortly after D-Day he took a company, headed by Diana Wynyard, in the play *Love from a Stranger* to France and Belgium, where he entertained the troops for several months. Returning to London, he went on another tour of England with *The Dancing Years* which played again to packed houses. It seemed that this musical could go on for ever in the provinces, and when Ivor left the cast to star in his new play *Perchance to Dream* it continued its tour year after year.

Perchance to Dream opened at the Hippodrome theatre in April 1945 and ran to the end of 1947 – this time more than a thousand performances. The war in the West ended soon after the opening and the victory celebrations brought a great boom to the theatre; the audiences at the Hippodrome were so enthusiastic that they cheered for half an hour when the show was over.

Although the plot of this musical was very complicated, spanning three periods of time, it was filled with romance and beauty. The action took place in a stately home of England and Ivor played a Regency buck, a Victorian composer and a twentieth-century musician. Muriel Barron, Margaret Rutherford and later Zena Dare co-starred with him. He had written a lovely score, and one song, *We'll Gather Lilacs* became the most popular piece that he had written since *Keep the Home Fires Burning*. It was, and for that matter still is, one of the great popular songs of our time.

When the play ended in London Ivor took it on a long and successful tour of South Africa.

However, through all these years of theatrical acclaim Ivor had suffered many personal sorrows; also his illness had weakened him and he never fully recovered his health.

*   *   *

In a life as successful and sunny as Ivor's, it would be giving a false impression to imply that no shadows ever fell, for indeed there was one incident (what a light word to apply to such a horrifying experience!) when Ivor was sentenced to a month's imprisonment in Wormwood Scrubs, the London jail whose name alone sends a shiver down the spine.

Ivor lived in a world of his own – the theatre – and he was a romantic; unfortunately there are people who romanticise in different ways. And that, plus Ivor's naturally trusting (even naïve) character, was the cause of what happened.

Under the wartime control of petrol, Ivor had an official permit to use his car to drive down to Redroofs to spend the weekends resting in order to get on with his work – which was considered important for morale – to say nothing of the work he did in entertaining the troops.

Suddenly the renewal of his permit was refused. Naturally upset, he remarked several times about the incident, often jokingly. But within earshot of Ivor's remarks was a young dedicated fan and friend of one of the members of his company who, while Ivor was on tour, kept turning up at the theatres where he was appearing.

Above: Ivor and Vanessa Lee in *King's Rhapsody.*

Right: Ivor and Vanessa Lee immediately after her success on the first night of *King's Rhapsody,* 1950.

74.
Above: Ivor (left) on holiday a
his Jamaican home with (nex
to him) Zena Dare (below
Olive Gilbert, Bobbie Andrew:
and (top right) two othe
friends.

75.
Above: Bobbie Andrews, Ivor,
Lord Beaverbrook and Bea-
trice Lillie at Ivor's home in
Jamaica. It was Ivor's last
holiday . . .

ove: Ivor Novello (left) arrives at the
ndon Law Courts on 16th May 1944 to
ar his appeal against his conviction of
ght weeks' imprisonment for conspiring to
mmit an offence against restriction on
e war-time use of cars. His appeal failed.
ny considered it a cruel and unjust
ntence.

ght: Ivor Novello (right) on his release
m prison on 12th June 1944. He resumed
s starring role in *The Dancing Years* at
e Adelphi Theatre, London on 20th June.

78.
Above left: The exterior of 'Redroofs', Ivor's famous home near Maidenhead, Berkshire.

79.
Above: Ivor in the pool at 'Redroofs' – standing in swimsuit (right) is actor Peter Graves, now Lord Graves, who married one of Ivor's leading ladies, Vanessa Lee.

80.
Left: A bathing party at 'Redroofs'. Ivor (sitting second from right), always the most generous of hosts, with some of his friends round the pool of his Berkshire home.

81.
Left: Ivor at a window c
'Redroofs'.

82.
Left: (l to r) Ivor, Alan Melvill
another friend, and Bobb
Andrews at 'Redroofs', 4
March 1951. He died two day
later.

Having heard about the car, she told him that the company she worked for would take it over, and a permit would be granted as they were engaged in war work. They had a branch in Reading and as Redroofs was on the direct route, he could be given a lift on Saturday nights, as the car would be going there in any case. It was all so easy!

Ivor made the weekend journey over a few months, then suddenly he had the shock of receiving a message from the managing director of the company saying that they had just found out about the transfer of the car to the company's name which they knew nothing about and had not authorised.

Of course the young lady's story was pure invention, and Ivor was eventually summoned to Bow Street magistrates' court, even though he had previously informed the authorities of the facts. He was sentenced to one month's imprisonment.

So Ivor Novello was condemned to the humiliation of prison garb, the black boredom of confinement in a cell, and all the sufferings which were so much more easily borne by the habitual criminals with whom he was surrounded.

He experienced deep despair at first, but the prison chaplain came to the rescue and invoked Ivor's help in the building of a new concert stage and in coaching, leading and playing the piano for the choir, which made a great deal of difference to the rest of his stay. What his public thought about the whole affair was demonstrated when on his release he returned to his role in *The Dancing Years* – there has never been so enthusiastic and emotional a reception in the London theatre. Ivor was back!

When I returned to England that summer, the thrill of being back in London, the city I loved most, was as great as when I had first come there twenty years before with Ivor. Outwardly, everything seemed the same to me; the ravages of the war years of bombing had disappeared but the wounds in the hearts of friends who had lost loved ones in the war could never be healed.

I went straight to the flat and found Ivor awaiting my arrival. We talked for hours, trying to catch up on the many things that had happened to us during the last ten years. He told me of his two tremendous successes *The Dancing Years* and *Perchance to Dream,* and now *King's Rhapsody* was the greatest of all. The advance sale of seats before it opened was fifty thousand pounds, a record for England and America up to that time. This showed what a multitude of theatregoers wanted to see a new Novello musical even before they had read the reviews.

He also had written and produced another musical, *Gay's the Word,* starring Cecily Courtneidge, which had opened in London and was playing to full houses, while four of his other musicals – *Glamorous Night, The Dancing Years, Careless Rapture* and *Perchance to Dream* were running simultaneously in England. It was an unprecedented triumph for a playwright-composer to have six musical productions playing at the same time.

Although he had retained his buoyant, youthful enthusiasm and his enormous capacity for enjoying life, Ivor showed signs, to those who knew him well, of the many sad blows he had suffered during the war years; they had left their imprint on him. He looked pale and tired, and he told me that he had worked terribly hard producing two big musicals at almost the same time, and needed a long rest, but he could not leave *King's Rhapsody* until later in the year when he hoped to go to his house in Jamaica and relax in the sun. He also told me that the past winter had been so cold that for five months he had left the flat only to drive to the theatre, act in the play, and then return home immediately. He felt he could never spend another winter in London.

We talked about the milestones in his career. He seemed to have almost forgotten about the score of films that he had made when he was the most popular film star in England; those days did not seem to be of interest to him anymore. He was proud of the plays he had written – fifteen in all – and the eight big-scale musicals he had written and composed. It seemed incredible that he was still in his fifties and had already given the public such a vast amount of entertainment. Certainly no man of the theatre in this century had achieved as much as he had.

190

He told me that he felt a continuous urge to create, that this drive to write and compose never left him, and that it was fortunate that he was happiest when he was working. He never could understand people who, because they came from wealthy or distinguished families, had no ambition to achieve something on their own.

The most amazing thing to me was that with all the fame and glory that had been showered on him Ivor had remained such a natural and unspoiled person. For over forty years his name had been known in every home in England, and yet he seemed completely unaware of the imact he had made on millions of people in his country. He had become a symbol of romance and glamour and his vivid personality had often overshadowed his plays, his acting and his music. Although now more active than at any time in his life, he had already become a legend.

When he went to his room to rest I opened the Guest Book and looked through the names of the people who had visited him during my long absence. It was like turning the pages of an international *Who's Who* – and the same was true of the Guest Book at Redroofs. The range of celebrities was extraordinary, not just theatrical but including royalty, heads of state, people from worlds quite beyond his own, united in friendship with a unique individual.

Ivor later told me that he had made a new will, and that after making provision for a few of his close friends he had left the bulk of his fortune and almost all of the royalties from his music to the four English theatrical charities. He was leaving Redroofs as a home for old actors and actresses in need of rest and country air. I thought how appropriately this would perpetuate his generosity to his own profession in the years to come.

That evening he had reserved seats for *King's Rhapsody* for Dorothy, two friends of ours from Rome, and myself, and later he was going to give a little supper party for us at the Caprice, a restaurant that he and some friends had financed for Mario of the Ivy.

Ivor had not exaggerated about *King's Rhapsody*. It was the best play that he had written – well constructed, dramatic, and with a generous sprinkling of comedy scenes. He had composed another beautiful score, somewhat lighter than *Glamorous Night* and *Careless Rapture*, but replete with lovely melodies. Christopher Hassall had again written the lyrics, and the songs, *Some Day my Heart will Awake*, *Fly Home*, *Little Heart* and *A Violin Begins to Play*, remain among the most beautiful numbers that he had composed. There was also some tzigany music in the Muranian ballet scene which was full of excitement and colour.

Like *Glamorous Night*, the play was set in a mythical Middle European kingdom, Murania, and told the story of a prince who, tiring of the political feuds in his country, goes to Paris with his mistress to live a life of freedom. When his father dies, he returns to his country and tries to rule wisely and justly. For political reasons he marries a princess of another country and later falls in love with her. The strong men in his government do not like the liberal way in which he is ruling the kingdom and force him to go into exile. When he hears that his little son is to be crowned king he cannot resist going back incognito to see the coronation and to have a last glimpse of his country.

The ingredients were those that Ivor knew his public loved so much – romance and glamour. He gave a mature and restrained performance, and the critics said it was his best since *Henry V*. For the role of the princess he had chosen Vanessa Lee, a beautiful young actress with a glorious voice, and he had made her his new star. She shone so brilliantly that she received a nightly ovation from the audiences. Zena Dare, as beautiful and elegant as ever, was the Queen Mother and had most of the witty lines in the play, and Phyllis Dare was charming in the part of the King's mistress. The coronation scene and the finale were as exquisite and emotional as anything Ivor had ever written, and with countless others I shall always remember them.

Our Italian friends enjoyed *King's Rhapsody* immensely and kept calling it an operetta. They said that in Italy the quality of the music and not the fact that a few actors spoke their lines instead of singing them determined the genre of the work. They told Ivor that his music was so beautiful that he must compose an opera, which I had been urging him to do since the success of *Glamorous Night.*

Ivor had arranged that on the next night we would go to see his other new play with music, *Gay's the Word.* This was a rollicking musical farce with Cecily Courtneidge presiding over the hilarious happenings. As a stage veteran turned schoolmistress, she had a wonderful opportunity of showing the talents which had made her one of the greatest comediennes on the English stage.

We spent the weekends at Redroofs which had retained the charm and personality that were to be found wherever Ivor lived. He always created an ambience of beauty, colour and comfort in his homes. Zena Dare, Dorothy Dickson, Phyllis Monkman, Isabel Jeans, Bea Lillie and many other great friends came down for weekends, and they all looked so happy, young, and beautiful that it made one wonder if the Fountain of Youth that Ponce de Leon was always searching for in America wasn't really to be found in the English countryside.

When summer had turned into autumn and the weather was becoming cold I realised, all too painfully, that the time had come for my reluctant departure, but as Ivor told me that I must spend every summer in England it was not a sad farewell like the one at the beginning of the war.

'You must come over every year in May and stay with us until October. We'll have many happy times together again at Redroofs,' he said as I made ready to return to Italy.

Finale

THE SUNSHINE WAS pouring into my hotel apartment in Rome. It was only the first week in March but the waiter who brought my breakfast said it was a summer day and that everybody was sitting at the tables outside the cafés.

I was beginning to dress hastily when the telephone rang and the operator told me that it was a call from London. A friend of mine had phoned to give me the tragic and totally unexpected news that Ivor had died during the night from a heart attack. I should not come to London, he said, as it was terribly cold and there was nothing I could do.

Slowly I put the telephone receiver in its place and sat down on a nearby chair. My mind seemed to have become a complete blank and I never have been able to remember the thoughts that passed through it. I was so stunned and griefstricken that I just sat there, bewildered and immobile, for a long time.

I began to feel very cold, in spite of the warmth in the rooms, and I put on a heavy sweater, a jacket and an overcoat, but I still remained chilled. I called for the waiter and ordered a large pot of hot coffee, and drank it down hurriedly. This seemed to pull me together, and my blood began to flow again. I was now completely aware of the tragedy that had befallen all of us who felt about Ivor as I did.

He had not had anything wrong with his heart before. What could have caused the trouble now? Then I remembered how pale and thin he had looked when I had seen him five months before. He said he had been working too hard and must have a rest, but despite this he had gone on playing in *King's Rhapsody* until the end. He had once said that he wanted to die on the stage just as the curtain was coming down on a brilliant success. His wish had almost come true.

In the late afternoon I went up to the terrace of the Casina Valadier in the Borghese Gardens as I had done so many times with Ivor to watch the sun set over Rome. The glorious day was bathed in sunshine and

194

low: The plaque in memory of Ivor
vello in St. Paul's Church (known as 'The
tors' Church'), Covent Garden, London.
e flowers – predominantly lilac – were
ced there by his life long friend and
ging star, Olive Gilbert.

Overleaf: The relief memorial sculpture
of Ivor Novello in St. Paul's Cathedral,
London.

IVOR NOVELLO
COMPOSER
1893-1951

groups of children were playing in the park. Some of them were standing in a circle, throwing a ball from hand to hand; others were playing an Italian version of Blind Man's Bluff while their elders kept a watchful eye on them.

The terrace was almost empty as it was too early in the year for the Romans to break their winter routine, but there were some cars parked by the iron railings and their owners were gazing at the view below them. As I walked to the terrace I passed an old couple, heavily clothed in grey and black woollens, sitting hand-in-hand on a small iron bench. They were huddled so close together, and seemed so nervous and timid, that they reminded me of two frightened little birds perched on the branch of a leafless tree. At times one of them whispered into the ear of the other and received a nod in response. I wondered how they had ever wandered so far from home, they seemed so weak and frail. Possibly they made a pilgrimage here every year to satisfy a nostalgia, or to celebrate a certain day of their youth, when they had pledged their love here.

On a nearby bench, a beautiful blonde girl and a handsome boy were sitting arm in arm, gazing into one another's eyes. Then the boy kissed the girl ardently on her face and neck, and she, responding, ran her fingers through his thick, black hair. They made a beautiful picture that seemed completely natural and a part of this wonderful spring day.

I walked over to the railing and gazed once more on the magnificent panorama that spread out before my eyes. There were the steeples and domes and the network of little streets that led from the Piazza di Spagna to the Corso, and beyond I could see the Castello St Angelo overlooking the Tiber, and the Victor Emanuel monument. One could just discern the Pantheon and the Coliseum, while in the background St Peter's Basilica stood out in all its eternal glory.

Slowly a beautiful yellow light settled over the city until it was bathed in gold, presaging the glorious sunset that was to follow. It was far too grandoise a scene for the mind to grasp all at once. Little wonder that the great painters and poets of every age had glorified this majestic sight in their paintings and in their poetry. This great city had been sacked, burned and destroyed but like the phoenix it had always risen again from its ashes. The Lord had sent Peter to build his church here and the first Popes and their courts had followed him. The thought of the millions of people who had been born, spent their lives, and died here during the centuries that had followed, and the great historical events of which they had formed a part, made one feel as small as a grain of sand in the great hourglass of time.

Suddenly, a sharp wind swept through the gardens. It was the famous *tramontana* which comes from the hills that surround Rome and gives warning that winter is not yet over, that this day has only been a brief herald of the spring that is still a month away.

The mothers and the nannies began to gather up their children, bundle them into their coats and hats, and hustle them off to their homes. The little old man and woman slowly rose to their feet, and still clutching each other closely trudged down the hill which leads to the church of Trinite del Monte. The terrace was empty now, except for the young girl and boy, who were locked in a passionate embrace.

I walked back to the hotel, calmed by the wonderful spectacle that I had just witnessed. Some words that Ivor had spoken when one of his best friends had died suddenly came to my mind. After days of sorrow, he had said, 'This won't do anyone any good at all. We must believe that she had to catch an early train. We'll take a later one and we'll all meet again at the next station.'

When I arrived in my rooms I found that the latest newspapers from London had been left under the door. I could read at a distance the large black headlines telling of Ivor's death. I put them quickly away in a desk drawer. I could not possibly have read them that day and I doubted if I would ever be able to. Then I knew what I wanted to do. I went to the cabinet where I kept my records and picked out my favourites from Ivor's musicals. I piled them on the gramophone, turned it on, and settled down in a comfortable chair. As the beautiful melodies from *Glamorous Night, Careless Rapture, The Dancing Years* and *King's Rhapsody* poured forth, the scenes and the people who played in them

198

flashed across my mind and I could see Ivor everywhere. He was standing on the deck of the boat with Mary Ellis, sitting on a roundabout with Dorothy Dickson, at the piano playing the enchanting music of *The Dancing Years.*

How could the papers have said that he was dead? For me he was living in every note of these haunting refrains. He had put so much of his heart and soul into creating this music that it had become a part of him, and he of it. Millions of people would listen to these melodies in the years to come, and they would be sung and played everywhere, as long as melody exists in this world.

Let us hope that this will be for ever, because history has told us that from the beginning of time man has always felt a great need of music to exalt him in times of happiness and to console him in times of sorrow.